Computers, Communication and Mental Models

This edition is dedicated to Professor Tom Gentry, lately of the Center for Telecommunications Courses, California State University, Stanislaus. His selfless concern for students and colleagues alike is sorely missed.

Computers, Communication and Mental Models

Edited by

DONALD L. DAY

School of Information Systems,
The University of New South Wales,
Sydney 2052, Australia
d.day@unsw.edu.au

DIANE K. KOVACS

Kovacs Consulting,
1117 Meadowbrook Boulevard,
Brunswick, Ohio 44212, USA
diane@kovacs.com

CRC Press
Taylor & Francis Group
Boca Raton London New York

CRC Press is an imprint of the
Taylor & Francis Group, an **informa** business

A TAYLOR & FRANCIS BOOK

First issued in hardback 2017

UK   Taylor & Francis Ltd, 2 Park Square, Milton Park, Abingdon, Oxon OX14 4RN
USA   Taylor & Francis Inc., 711 Third Avenue, New York, NY 10017

British Library Cataloguing in Publication Data
A catalogue record for this book is available from the British Library.

ISBN 13: 978-1-138-41397-9 (hbk)
ISBN 13: 978-0-7484-0543-5 (pbk)

Library of Congress Cataloguing in Publication Data are available

A previous edition of work presented here was published in the *Electronic Journal on Virtual Culture*, **2**(2), 16 May 1994, (http://rdz.stjohns.edu/ejvc/ejvc.html).

Cover design by Hybert Design & Type
Typeset by Solidus (Bristol) Limited

Contents

About the Editors   vi

Preface: Computerised tools as intermediaries in the communication   vii
     of mental maps

Part 1: The Communication Process

1.   Human-computer-human interaction: how computers affect   11
    interpersonal communication
    Rodney Fuller

2.   Designing for cognitive communication: epistemic fidelity or   15
    mediating collaborative inquiry?
    Jeremy Roschelle

3.   Computer-mediated interpersonal communication: the HCHI approach   28
    Lajos Balint

Part 2: Knowledge Representation

4.   Mapping the mapper   37
    John Wood and Paul Taylor

5.   Mapping spatial cognition with computers   45
    Phil Moose, Teri Stueland, Krista Kern and Tom Gentry

Part 3: Cooperative Work

6.   The world view of collaborative tools   57
    Munir Mandviwalla

7.   Computer-based simulation models for problem-solving: 67
    communicating problem understandings
    Ray Paul and Peter Thomas

8.   The effects of combining interactive graphics and text in   74
    computer-mediated small group decision-making
    Jozsef Toth

Postscript: A convergence of disciplines   88

Index   89

About the Editors

DONALD L. DAY is a senior lecturer in the School of Information Systems at The University of New South Wales, Sydney. His interests in computers, communications and mental models stem from prior careers in software engineering and magazine editing, as well as from studies at The University of Missouri (journalism and speech), The American University (international studies) and Syracuse University (information transfer). Dr. Day's current research involves both the behavioural responses of users to constraints in computerised design tools and the cultural bases of user acceptance of information technology. He currently is a member of the Human Sciences Special Editorial Board of the journal *Interacting with Computers*.

DIANE K. KOVACS is an experienced Internet and World Wide Web training consultant. She is Editor-in-Chief of the *Electronic Journal on Virtual Culture*. Ms. Kovacs is also Editor-in-Chief of the *Directory of Scholarly Electronic Conferences* (published in print by the Association of Research Libraries) and co-moderator of Libref-L (Discussion of Library Reference Issues) and of GovDoc-L (Discussion of Government Documents Issues). Currently, she is adjunct Assistant Professor in the School of Library and Information Science, Kent State University. Diane Kovacs has written and spoken frequently about scholarly resources on academic networks. She has also taught workshops about using Internet Resources for scholarly research, for more than five years. She is president and CEO of Kovacs Consulting, an Internet consulting firm.

Preface

Computerised tools as intermediaries in the communication of mental maps

Every time the developers of software packages decide to implement an approach, a preferred process, or a set of options, they communicate favoured world views to all users of their products. The ways in which software leverages and colours users' efforts makes developers' design decisions critical to the productivity, effectiveness and work satisfaction of users.

In particular, software tools (such as CASE) shape user cognition, by communicating the perspectives and biases of developers to users. Computers thereby are powerful in their ability to channel activities and perspectives in an almost unlimited range of environments.

It has been said that to a man with a hammer, every problem looks like a nail. The capabilities of the tool at hand filter the appearance of the problem. Once Whorf (1952) had suggested that language colours human experience, tools and their potential to modify perception could be seen as key in the use of technology to deal with the environment. In the sense meant here, mental models constructed by software developers and computer users are analogous to the linguistic schema built by individuals to interpret and relate experiences in the real world.

In this collection of papers from a wide variety of disciplines, the unifying thread is the ability of computers as tools to communicate world views -- ways of understanding and grappling with the environment -- from tool developers to tool users.

The unique aspect of software tools that sets them apart from most (perhaps all) past extensions of human skill and perception is that they communicate cognition between human beings via a programmable electronic medium. As a result, these tools are infinitely flexible -- the first known example (other than the humble Swiss army knife) of an implement that can be made to fit the problem, rather than vice versa. This *cognitive fit* (or lack thereof) is an important aspect of how computerised tools are applied and understood (Day, 1995).

The use of computerised tools as intermediaries in the communication of mental maps represents a change in kind in the way people deal with their environments.

The concept of *intermediaries* is drawn primarily from information science. There, it represents skilled technical specialists who interpret user queries to complex database

systems, to ensure efficient retrieval of relevant documents or other artefacts. An "intermediary" in this sense is someone or something which bridges a gap between an individual needing information and the source of that information.

The concept of *mental maps* comes from cognitive psychology, which attempts to explain how and why individuals rely on structured mental representations of the real world to deal with external stimuli. Such mental models allow stereotypical responses to entire classes of stimuli, considerably reducing the mental workload of everyday life.

Essentially, three types of communication are involved in computerised tools: Communication between tool developers and tool users, communication between tool users and tool developers, and communication among tool users. All three are represented in the eight papers presented here. Although implemented in highly complex systems -- some including artificial intelligence components -- the fundamental concept embodied is simple: Tools originally designed as extensions of human skills and talents in fact filter the act of communication in ways far in excess of the influence that the term "tools" normally conveys.

Contributions

The eight papers in this book are organised into three broadly defined groups. Included are three chapters that focus on the communication process, two that address knowledge representation, and three that examine computer-supported cooperative work.

The communication process

The impact of electronic communication upon users' mental models of each other is addressed by **Rodney Fuller**. Rodney finds that electronic mail users consistently perceive their correspondents to be more analytical and judgmental than the correspondents themselves believe they are. He also finds that such effects do not exist in subjects who have met face-to-face but have not communicated electronically.

Jeremy Roschelle addresses the *mis*communication of physics concepts from experts to students via computers. It is not enough, Jeremy says, to represent concepts with high fidelity. A mismatch in mental models held by experts vs. learners may prevent learners from assimilating target knowledge effectively. Jeremy advocates a mediated collaborative inquiry (MCI) approach, in which representations external to the expert-learner interaction mediate communication. Using MCI, learners may construct, negotiate and maintain shared interpretations that allow them to participate increasingly in the expert community's practices of representation.

The role of intelligent machines in bridging gaps in mental models is explored by **Lajos Balint**. A sufficiently capable computer, Lajos says, should translate, formalise, analyse and re-synthesise human-to-human communications. Such machines would need to capitalise upon knowledge of communicating individuals' mental models to make adjustments to messages exchanged (thereby ensuring content fidelity).

Knowledge representation

John Wood and **Paul Taylor** describe a novel hypertext environment which helps researchers and students of art and design map information into a multi-dimensional network, thereby developing meaningful mental models of interrelationships from disparate domains.

The design philosophy of Buckminster Fuller is the target information. By navigating through Fuller's work, users become aware of the issue of mapping itself, and are sensitised to the mapping process which individuals undergo during human-computer interaction.

Fractal geometry, digital video technology and research on spatial cognition are combined as **Moose et al** explore the structure of mental maps. Pointing behaviours and digitised sketch maps are used to study individual differences and the dynamic properties of mental models. The authors propose that the fractal dimensions of pointing behaviour may model mental constructs that are applied during brain processing of sensory data.

Cooperative work

Munir Mandviwalla describes relationships among the most common world views held by developers of collaborative tools. Munir uses Adaptive Structuration Theory to examine developers' world views and to outline the potential of such views to influence users. He also investigates the feasibility of matching world views to users and of developing tools to support multiple world views.

The effective communication of problem understandings among users of group decision support systems (GDSS) is the concern of **Ray Paul** and **Peter Thomas**. Their chapter describes computer-based tools that apply dynamic simulation models to improve the communication of problem understanding. Ray and Peter examine the bases of the mental model concept, which they argue should be expanded to include the ways in which computer technology is embedded in complex contexts, designer and user activities, and tasks.

Finally, **Jozsef Toth** examines the use of graphics in a discussion-oriented GDSS setting. Joe finds that summary graphics significantly affect the process and outcome of choice-dilemma decision-making tasks. He also observes that varying the form of information displayed can either augment or attenuate normative and informational forms of social influence. (If graphics are included, the first discussant to advocate a position has a significantly stronger influence on the group than if only text is displayed).

Credits

This book began as a special (theme) issue of a fledgling electronic journal, the *Electronic Journal On Virtual Culture*. Conventional wisdom holds that electronic journals (like electronic newspapers, magazines, movies and correspondence) are the wave of the future.

In any event, electronic journals are very new players in the academic marketplace of ideas. As a result, it is difficult to attract authors. This is due in part to the fact that restrictions intrinsic to the medium (e.g., ascii-only formatting) make developing a paper for the electronic medium more frustrating than for print publication.

Prestige is another major problem faced by electronic journals. Academics categorise potential outlets according to the perceived impact of having one's work published in a particular journal. A significant factor in judgments of prestige is the rigour of the review process. Because some electronic journals conduct no peer review (and others, including the *EJVC*, contain both reviewed and non-reviewed material), authors (and promotion and tenure committees) are sceptical about quality of scholarship.

This scepticism led in the *EJVC* special issue to a strong emphasis on review procedures that are every bit as rigorous as for any print journal. First, most papers were double-blind reviewed by three or more individuals (two submissions received only two reviews each). Several reviewers (Table 1) were recognised authorities in their fields, with experience reviewing submissions for leading print journals. The review board included practitioners from industry as well as academics. If a submission required major revisions after its first-pass review, revised papers were reviewed again by at least one previously critical reviewer, before being accepted for publication.

Credit also is due to Jane Carey (Arizona State University West, U.S.A.), Pierrette Bergeron (University of Montreal, Canada), and Pertti Jaarvinen (University of Tampere, Finland) for distributing the call for papers.

Table 1. Reviewers of *Computers, Communication & Mental Models*

Ben Anderson	Loughborough University of Technology	U.K.
Andrew Cohill	Virginia Tech	U.S.A.
Elizabeth Dykstra-Erickson	US West	U.S.A.
Douglas Gordin	Northwestern University	U.S.A.
Rachelle Heller	George Washington University	U.S.A.
Munir Mandviwalla	Temple University	U.S.A.
John Murray	University of Michigan	U.S.A.
Max North	Georgia Tech	U.S.A.
Jacob Palme	Stockholm University	Sweden
Frank Ritter	University of Nottingham	U.K.
Bob Root	Bellcore	U.S.A.
Jacques Verville	Syracuse University	U.S.A.
Yvonne Waern	Linkoeping University	Sweden
Marilyn Welles	Mitre Corporation	U.S.A.

Note: Affiliations shown are those at the time of the original *EJVC* release (May 1994).

Donald L. Day
Sydney, Australia

Diane K. Kovacs
Brunswick, Ohio

March 1996

References

DAY, D. 1995, "Adaptive discovery and least commitment: an extension of cognitive fit". In Hasan, H. & Nicastri, C. (eds), *HCI: A Light into the Future*, 256-261. Proceedings, 4th conference of the Computer Human Interaction Special Interest Group of the Ergonomics Society of Australia (OZCHI'95), Nov. 27-30, Wollongong, NSW.

WHORF, B. 1952, *Collected Papers on Metalinguistics*. Foreign Service Institute, Dept. of State, Washington.

Part 1: The Communication Process

1

Human-computer-human interaction: how computers affect interpersonal communication

RODNEY FULLER

Bellcore, 444 Hoes Lane, Piscataway, NJ 08854 USA
fuller@ctt.bellcore.com

Abstract. There are two contemporary paradigms of the human-computer interface (HCI) -- the conversation paradigm and the direct manipulation paradigm. Neither of these paradigms provides a good model for designers of electronic communication media. A paradigm based on use of the computer as a medium for conversation (rather than as the target of conversation) might resolve this problem. With this paradigm, users of electronic communication media may be less likely to mis-perceive other users' personalities.

Two groups of subjects were tested for their abilities to make personality assessments of people they had communicated with. The first group of paired subjects were users of traditional electronic communication media. Each pair consisted of Person A, who took the test as if s/he were someone (Person B) s/he had communicated with but had never seen, and Person B, who took the same test describing him- or herself. A second group of paired subjects who had never communicated using electronic media were asked to perform the same tasks. The electronic media group consistently perceived the person they communicated with to be more analytical (p < .003) and judgmental (p < .03) than that person perceived him- or herself as being. There were no significant differences in perception within the face-to-face (no electronic contact) group.

1. Introduction

1.1 *Contemporary design paradigms*

Two contemporary design paradigms exist under the human-computer interface (HCI) umbrella: the human-computer conversation paradigm, and the direct manipulation paradigm. As Moran and Anderson (1990, p. 381) note

> The HCI banner is used to cover a wide range of interests and topics, but it usually refers to an individual human [-computer] user interacting with a computer work station.... It is often thought of in terms of a con-

versation paradigm in which the user converses with the machine.

The more recent "direct manipulation" paradigm posits that the user interacts directly with the environment, using the computer as a tool (Moran and Anderson, 1990; Shneiderman, 1992). Although these two HCI paradigms satisfy the design needs of a vast majority of contemporary computer applications, they may not be the most appropriate paradigms for all applications. One of these ill-served applications is that of electronic communication media (electronic mail and bulletin boards). The design focus for electronic media views the computer as a medium for conversation between users, rather than as a dialogue partner with the user.

This change in design focus (from object of action to medium for communicating action and intent) creates a new level of complexity for the designer of electronic communication media. It is well known that the selection of a data representation places an upper limit on the complexity of what can be modelled, as well as making some elemental forms of interaction ambiguous (Shannon and Weaver, 1963; Cover and Thomas, 1991). This creates special concerns for the electronic media designer because although the human-computer interaction itself may be unambiguous, the complexity of the communication may overwhelm the medium (Sproull and Kiesler, 1986).

In terms of the paradigm shift between conversation only and manipulation, Frank Ludolph (a Xerox Alto/Star and Apple Macintosh designer) has said

> As to paradigm shifting from workbench to communicator, I'm not sure that the latter precludes the former. Perhaps the communicator is just a tool on the workbench? To fully shift to communicator, the workbench

work would likely be performed by the computer as an intelligent agent that an individual communicates with. A full shift would effectively turn an individual into a paraplegic, incapable of dealing with the world directly. I think that the best path is co-existence of the two paradigms.

(Personal communication, January 9, 1991).

If the two paradigms -- human-computer interaction (HCI) and human-computer-human interaction (HCHI) -- are to coexist, then guidelines for combining them need to be created. But before guidelines can be developed, we need measures that will indicate how effectively the paradigm in fact models the behaviour of those interaction participants. One possible measure -- the use of social cognitions to assess the effectiveness of communication behaviour -- is investigated here.

1.2 *Electronic communication and mental models*

Electronic mail and bulletin board services are two common types of electronic media. Electronic mail (e-mail) probably is the more common. It consists of transmitting text from one computer user to another, as if it were a letter. Because electronic messages are intended for another person's use, e-mail can be thought of as facilitating human-computer-human interaction (HCHI).

An interesting characteristic of communication via electronic media is that it allows for differences between design structures and social interaction to be studied, as part of the process of using tools to convey shared meaning. For example, users of electronic media sometimes communicate with colleagues whom they have never met. If these interactions continue over a period of time, the participants usually develop mental pictures of what their correspondents are like. It is not uncommon to meet someone you have been communicating with via e-mail for several years, only to realise that they are entirely different from what you had expected. This is an example of a "breakdown" in communication (Heidegger, 1962).

Winograd and Flores (1986) describe *breakdown* as the invention of a network of understanding that is incorrect and private -- an understanding that cannot be shared, and that inhibits communication. Because of the limitations imposed on communication by the nature of electronic media (typically, only text documents can be sent, with little chance for an interactive conversation), the fact that communications break down is not surprising.

If one person's mental model is highly discrepant from another person's, a breakdown will occur. The models of other peoples' expectations and prior knowledge that we bring into communication can influence not only the tone of the discussion, but also our own expectations of someone else's personality. Such models can influence communication patterns and styles of the person sending a message.

Recent work regarding the effect that social cognitions (judgments, attitudes, and stereotypes) have on an individual's communication patterns has shown that people can mis-communicate in predictable ways, depending upon the model or stereotype they employ (Fiske and Taylor, 1991). While it may be possible to coexist electronically without ever facing a breakdown in expectations, even small discrepancies in communication models become apparent when individuals talk face-to-face.

By measuring the perceptions of correspondents' personality traits held by participants who communicate frequently by electronic media (but who have never met), then comparing such judgments to the correspondents' perceptions of their own personality traits, we can identify tendencies towards common perceptual differences. If such tendencies do follow common patterns and if users of electronic media appear to develop certain types of misperceptions more often than others, knowledge of these effects could be helpful in the creation of pragmatic guidelines for construction of electronic media systems.

2. Method

The Myers-Briggs Inventory is a short, well known personality inventory that has high reliability on several basic dimensions. It has been used before in HCI to test the styles applied by computer programmers (Shneiderman 1980, Tognazzini 1992). A shorter test modelled after Myers-Briggs was developed by Keirsey and Bates (1978). While the reliability of this shorter version is unknown, due to its length it is more feasible to administer via questionnaire. Both instruments produce scores on four dichotomous sub-scales: introversion-extroversion, intuition-sensation, thinking-feeling, and judging-perceiving. These four sub-scales are combined to indicate personality "type".

Four hundred fifty Keirsey and Bates tests (questionnaires) were distributed to two groups: (a) people who took the test as if they were a co-worker whom they knew only through e-mail (the "e-mail only" group) and (b) people who took the test as if they were a co-worker with whom they had *never* communicated using e-mail (the "face-to-face" group).

For the e-mail only group, 200 tests were distributed at random to members of the Cognitive Science Society (a multi-disciplinary group). Two hundred more tests were distributed at random to attendees of the 1990 Conference on Computer-Supported Cooperative Work. For both groups, only people who listed e-mail addresses in the United States were solicited. Respondents were asked to identify someone whom they had communicated with, but with whom they were personally unacquainted. They were to complete the test imagining that they were this other (targeted) person.

In the face-to-face group, 28 graduate students and 22 employees at a retail outlet were asked to identify someone they had worked with but with whom they had never communicated electronically. The same questionnaire then was sent to the people who had been identified (targeted) by the graduate students and employees. This second group was asked to complete the questionnaire as if they were themselves.

After these measures were obtained for each pair of participants (one person taking the test as if s/he were someone else, and the someone else taking it as his- or herself), scores were compared to assess whether users of electronic media are more likely to develop certain types of mis-perceptions, more often.

3. Results

Ninety-three questionnaires were returned from the original mailing of 450. In the e-mail only group, 60 tests were returned initially, 30 of which were returned blank with notes explaining that the respondents did not communicate with anyone whom they did not know personally. Fourteen of the remaining e-mail only questionnaires were returned after a follow-up mailing. Thirty-three questionnaires were returned initially by face-to-face participants; 26 more were returned due to a second mailing. (See Table 1.)

Table 1. Experimental design and response rates

Respondent Type	Response Rate N	Response Rate %	Usable Rate N	Usable Rate %
A (original)				
e-mail only	60	15	30	7.5
FTF	33	66	33	66
A' (targeted)				
e-mail only	14	3.5	14	3.5
FTF	26	52	26	52

Note: Half of respondents in the e-mail only group do not communicate with anyone they don't know personally.

Responses were allocated to the 4 sub-scales: introversion-extroversion, sensation-intuition, thinking-feeling, and perceiving-judging (see Table 2).

Correlations of the sub-scales between participants in the e-mail only group exhibited two significant differences. The original respondents were more likely to rate targeted respondents higher on the thinking sub-scale (and lower on the feeling scale) than were targeted respondents themselves ($r = .83$, $p < .003$). Original respondents also were more likely to rate targeted respondents as being more judgmental (and less perceiving) than the targeted respondents rated themselves ($r = .60$, $p < .03$).

For the face-to-face group, no significant differences were found between perceptions of paired respondents.

Table 2. Means and standard deviations of the e-mail only group

	Mean	Standard Deviation
Introversion		
Original respondent	4.23	2.59
Targeted respondent	4.50	2.01
Extroversion		
Original respondent	5.77	2.59
Targeted respondent	5.50	2.01
Sensation		
Original respondent	9.27	4.30
Targeted respondent	9.38	4.30
Intuition		
Original respondent	10.73	4.30
Targeted respondent	10.63	4.30
Thinking		
Original respondent	11.38	4.69
Targeted respondent	10.70	4.69
Feeling		
Original respondent	8.63	4.69
Targeted respondent	9.29	4.69
Perceiving		
Original respondent	9.48	5.07
Targeted respondent	7.56	3.25
Judging		
Original respondent	10.53	5.07
Targeted respondent	12.44	3.25

4. Discussion

Findings suggest that users of electronic media develop consistent mis-perceptions across several personality dimensions when judging individuals they communicate with, but whom they have not met in person. Their mis-perceptions contrast markedly with a lack of perceptual differences among people who have met face-to-face. This contrast indicates either that people are not using electronic media as it was conceived or that the technology limits the quality of communication that can take place between participants (possibly due to limited bandwidth).

Another finding is the fact that half the original e-mail only participants mentioned explicitly that they do not communicate with anyone they do not know personally. This lack of "e-mail only" relationships is especially surprising since the majority of participants were computer or cognitive scientists, who might be presumed to be comfortable with computer-based media. Although this study does not address the reasons why so many fail to maintain relationships based solely on electronic communication, this surprising result may lead to commercial development of more semantic human-computer communication models for electronic media (see Targowski and Bowman, 1988). It remains to be seen whether such future systems, designed to prevent predicable breakdowns during e-mail use, will in fact result in an increase in relationships maintained only through electronic media.

In summary, this study demonstrates that social cognitions can be used to measure the effective bandwidth of electronically mediated conversations, as implied by the fidelity of perceptions formed. The use of Myers-Briggs tests and other similar measures can provide designers of future electronic media with guidelines for combining today's conversation and direct manipulation paradigms to produce tomorrow's communication paradigm.

Acknowledgment

This research was supported partially by the Jenness Hannigan Research Fellowship.

References

COVER, T.M. AND THOMAS, J.A. 1991, *Elements of Information Theory.* (Wiley & Sons, New York).

FISKE, S.T. AND TAYLOR, S.E. 1991, *Social Cognition* (2d ed). (McGraw-Hill, New York).

HEIDEGGER, M. 1962, *Being and Time.* (Harper & Row, New York).

KEIRSEY, D. AND BATES, M. 1978, *Please Understand Me.* (Prometheus Nemesis Book Co., Del Mar, CA).

MORAN, T.P. AND ANDERSON, R.J. 1990, The workaday world as a paradigm for CSCW design. *Proceedings, Conference on Computer-Supported Cooperative Work*, October 7-10. Los Angeles. (ACM, New York).

SHANNON, C.E. AND WEAVER, W. 1963, *The Mathematical Theory of Communication.* (Univ. of Illinois Press, Urbana, IL).

SHNEIDERMAN, B. 1980, *Software Psychology: Human factors in Computer and Information Systems.* (Winthrop Publishers, Cambridge, MA).

SHNEIDERMAN, B. 1992, *Designing the User Interface: Strategies for Effective Human-Computer Interaction* (2d ed). Addison-Wesley, Reading, MA).

SPROULL, L. AND KEISLER, S. 1986, Reducing social context cues: electronic mail in organizational communications. *Management Science,* **32**, 1492-1512.

TARGOWSKI, A.S. AND BOWMAN, J.P. 1988, The layer-based, pragmatic model of the communication process. *The Journal of Business Communication,* **25**, 5-24.

TOGNAZZINI, B. 1992, *Tog on Interface.* Addison-Wesley, Reading, MA).

WINOGRAD T. AND FLORES, C.F. 1986, *Understanding Computers and Cognition: A New Foundation for Design.* (Addison-Wesley, Reading, MA).

2

Designing for cognitive communication: epistemic fidelity or mediating collaborative inquiry?

JEREMY ROSCHELLE

SimCalc Project, 4104 24th St #344, San Francisco CA 94114 USA
jeremy@dewey.soe.berkeley.edu

Abstract. This article examines the generalisation of the mental model principle to communication of a system of concepts across world views. I use an example of an educational simulation designed to teach physics concepts to examine such communication and to illustrate two design perspectives.

Gaps between world views prevent students from interpreting displays literally, and thus limit the extent to which communication can be achieved by representing knowledge accurately. Hence, rather than merely representing mental models accurately, designers must focus on supporting communicative practices. I suggest four specific design principles within a mediated collaborative inquiry perspective.

1. Introduction

> Intentions are fairly easy to perceive, but frequently
>   do not come about and are not fulfilled.
> Design is hard to perceive. But it is design and
>   not intention that creates the future.

(Boulding, 1985, p. 212)

Software should be designed to support the user's mental model of how the system operates (Young, 1981; Kieras & Bovair, 1984; Tauber & Ackermann, 1990, 1991; Norman, 1991). For example, a graphic user interface (GUI) desktop helps users learn computer filing systems by supporting a direct manipulation model analogous to a familiar, physical desktop (Smith, Irby, Kimball, & Verplank, 1982).

This article examines the generalisation of the mental model principle to communication of a system of concepts across world views. By building a computational model, educators often intend to communicate difficult concepts, enabling students to learn science, mathematics, history or another subject more easily. This generalisation extends the original mental model principle in two ways.

First, in the general case, the target knowledge is *embodied* in computation, but is not necessarily *about* a computer system. The GUI desktop is a model of a computer's filing system. In contrast, in the example used in this chapter, students learn about the concepts of velocity and acceleration. These concepts are not generally involved in the operation of a computer system.

Second, in the generalised case, learners cannot readily assimilate target knowledge to their current world view. Thus, whereas the GUI desktop is a natural extension of an office worker's existing model, in the example used in this chapter, communication requires that students cross the gap between their view and scientists' view of physics concepts.

Dynamic and visual computer displays offer the possibility of enhancing communication about concepts across world views, but also raise a difficult issue: How can computer representations be used to communicate a system of concepts to a student who does not already participate in the expert's world view? Answering this question requires considering the relation between a designer's intentions and students' learning processes. How are external representations related to the knowledge that students construct?

In one view, external representations denote concepts, constraints, or models that learners seek to decode and internalise (Reddy, 1979). A design is assumed to be superior if the external representation portrays the expert's mental model with high fidelity -- with accuracy and clarity, and without ambiguity or extraneous noise. Henceforth, this approach will be called "epistemic fidelity" (Wenger, 1987): It focuses attention on the fidelity of an external display with respect to an expert's mental model.

Using a case study of the "Envisioning Machine" (EM),

an educational simulation that is intended to help students learn physics concepts, I will expose the fallacy of assuming that a high fidelity model will lead to appropriate knowledge structures in a learner's head. In fact, students often do not know what to do, where to look, or how to make sense of a visual display in order to internalise external models correctly. Thus, students do not perceive the design in accordance with the designers' intentions.

This is a symptom of the disjunction between newcomer and expert world views (Clancey, 1989). In particular, extensive research has documented the depth of the disjunction between science students and professional scientists (Carramazza, McCloskey, & Green, 1981; Halhoun & Hestenes, 1985; McDermott, 1984). The gap between students' and scientists' world views is not localised at the level of "concepts" and "misconceptions," but extends throughout the fabric of thinking -- including perception, focus of attention, descriptions of the world, practices of interactions with the world, forms of valid knowledge, and values. Artefacts cannot form a conduit that passes "mental models" across the gap between expert and newcomer world views.

In an alternative view, external representations mediate interaction through which learners construct and maintain shared interpretations. External representations can constitute a physical backdrop against which learners coordinate communicative acts so as to increasingly participate in a community's practice of representation use (Lave & Wenger, 1989). Learning occurs through a social process of inquiry (Dewey, 1938) that occurs as students create, negotiate and try out meanings for the activity in which they are engaged. I call this alternative perspective "mediated collaborative inquiry" (Roschelle, 1992a), because it focuses on the role of design as providing a medium that supports communicative practices which enable meanings to be shared.

The mediated collaborative inquiry (MCI) perspective differs from a high fidelity perspective in three major ways.

First, the design goals are different. MCI design focuses on the resolution of ambiguities and differences in interpretation (Roschelle & Clancey, 1992). In contrast, the epistemic fidelity point of view assumes that communication and internalisation can be unproblematic if the relationship between the display and the target mental model is made precise.

Second, in the epistemic fidelity view, the main axis of interaction is between the computer and user. In the MCI view, the main axis of interaction is among people, with the computer model providing common ground to act upon and talk about (Teasley & Roschelle, 1993).

Third, whereas the epistemic fidelity view seeks to enable learning by representing knowledge or embodying models, the MCI view seeks to enable learning by supporting communicative practices. This view highlights the importance of designing resources that help people manage the uncertainty of interpretation that occurs inevitably when learners interact with expert representations.

Much has been written about the difference between conventional teaching and collaborative inquiry based teaching (e.g. Johnson & Johnson, 1987; Slavin, 1990). Herein, I focus on the significance of this change for the design of computer displays. I suggest four specific design principles within a mediated collaborative inquiry perspective:

o   Extending engagement with the problematic situation,
o   Supporting focus and context,
o   Enabling communicative action, and
o   Learning by doing.

These directly relate to needs that arise when conversational participants attempt to construct shared meanings that span world views.

2. The Envisioning Machine

The EM (Roschelle, 1991) is a direct manipulation graphical simulation of the scientific concepts of velocity and acceleration. It is intended to be a tool for beginning physics students at the level of middle school through first year university. The EM screen is divided into two windows: the "Observable World" and the "Newtonian World." The Observable World displays a ball (a black circle) and the Newtonian World displays a particle (a white circle). The thin arrow with its base at the particle's center represents the particle's velocity vector. The thick arrow with its base at the velocity's tip represents the particle's acceleration. Students control the simulation using a menu of commands.

When the simulation is run, the computer displays an animation of both the particle and of the ball moving across the screen. During the computer simulation, both the particle and the ball leave a series of trace dots behind them as they move, placing the dots at a uniform rate. These dots therefore contain information about the objects' speed, as well as its path. All the motions displayed by the EM are at constant velocity or constant acceleration.

2.1 *Inspiration for the EM design*

The inspiration for the original EM design grew from research on physicists' use of mental models. By "mental model," I mean the capability to predict the behaviour of a complex system by mentally simulating changes in the state of the system over time according to the logic of the system's component processes (Johnson-Laird, 1983; Gentner & Stevens, 1983; Jih & Reeves, 1992).

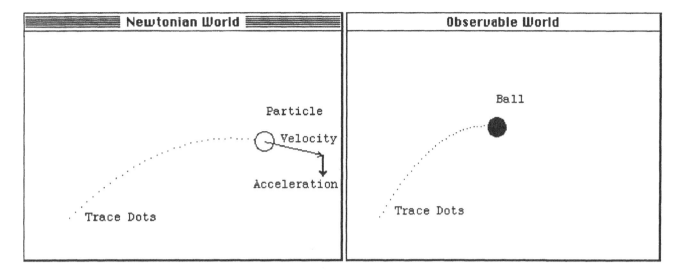

Figure 1. The Envisioning Machine (labels added)

In one study of mental models (Roschelle & Greeno 1987), we presented experts in physics with diagrams of physical situations and asked simply, "What's happening?" The resulting think-aloud protocol revealed that experts reasoned about physical situations by creating two parallel mental models, one which represented objects corresponding to physical reality and the other which represented objects corresponding to abstract scientific principles. Physicists developed their analyses of physical situations by comparing the predictions of both mental models.

The initial goal of the EM project was to implement a graphic, direct manipulation computer simulation that externalised physicists' dual mental models. The EM "Observable World" window was intended to correspond to an expert's mental model of a physical situation; the EM "Newtonian World" was intended to correspond to an expert's mental model of abstract scientific principles.

The EM presents visual images that neither students nor physicists have ever seen before. The representation of velocity and acceleration vectors as arrows is common practice. The EM extends previous displays of this representation by presenting the arrows as animate objects that register their values in time. As the particle moves across the screen, the velocity and acceleration vectors show the instantaneous velocity and acceleration. This real-time display represents the values of position, velocity, and acceleration changing over time, corresponding to their defined meaning. Previous static diagrams could not show changes over time. They could only represent such changes in space (for example, in a graph).

2.2 *Design rationale*

The original EM design was guided by two principles: An overall metaphor of scientific visualisation, and a specific emphasis on epistemic fidelity.

The scientific visualisation metaphor guided many design choices. One example is the choice of representation. Velocity and acceleration can be represented in many forms:

o   as lists of numbers (i.e., v = [10 20]),
o   as graphs of their value versus time, and
o   as arrows.

The list of numbers was rejected because it is too limited to represent an expert mental model.

The EM does not use the graph representation for two reasons: First, although a graph is good for representing measurements of values, it is bad for direct manipulation -- students would have difficulty setting velocity and acceleration. Second, although graphs are good for representing a one-dimensional motion, it is difficult to visualise a two-dimensional motion from a graph.

Instead, the EM uses the vector representation, for three reasons:

o   the vector representation is important in physicists' mental models,
o   it is easy to implement direct manipulation, and
o   it can represent two dimensional motions gracefully.

Even within this specification, further representational choices are necessary. One choice is whether to represent the concepts as "x" and "y" components, or as a single vector. EM uses a representation of velocity and acceleration as single vectors.

Another choice is among the forms of acceleration: constant acceleration, impulse acceleration, and uniform circular acceleration. While each reduces to the same set of definitions, the three forms of acceleration correspond to qualitatively different motions: They would require different direct manipulation interfaces.

Within the scientific visualisation metaphor, a dominant

rationale for the remaining EM design choices was epistemic fidelity. A good example of high fidelity design is the choice of scaling factors for the velocity and acceleration vectors. While the vectors could be scaled to arbitrary sizes (i.e., multiplied by a constant when converting from the arrow representation to real-time motion), the length of the velocity arrow in the EM is scaled to correspond exactly to the change of position that would occur over one second of constant velocity motion. This scaling reifies the meaning of velocity as change of position, because the tip of the velocity points to the place that velocity will be in one second.

Figure 2. Differences in placement of the
acceleration vector

A more controversial choice in the EM is the placement of the acceleration vector at the tip of the velocity vector. This placement emphasises the causal relationship among position, velocity and acceleration: velocity changes position and acceleration changes velocity. Thus, velocity is attached to the center position of the particle and acceleration is attached to the velocity. Under a high fidelity assumption, this representation should make the relationships among position, velocity, and acceleration more obvious. A more conventional representation, however, attaches acceleration to the center position of the particle.

3. Lessons about epistemic fidelity

Everyone agrees that people learn from experience. It is considerably less common to question what experience looks like from a students' point of view. Typically, educators and researchers assume that by describing the objects and relations that a knowledgeable observer would see in physical materials, they have described the experience that students have.

In my research, 10 pairs of high school students were videotaped as they used the EM collaboratively for several hours. The students had no prior knowledge of physics. Their goal was to discover how to set the velocity and acceleration vectors in the Newtonian World window in order to match motions in the Observable World. In each of two sessions, the students were given 10 Observable World motions to match. At the end of each session they were interviewed. Following both sessions, students were given a multiple-choice test that checks for a correct understanding of velocity and acceleration, and probes for common misconceptions.

Through the interviews and a detailed analysis of the students' videotaped problem solving performance and talk, I identified three categories of knowledge that students developed. Based on these categories, I constructed a description of how students experience the EM. In order to calibrate this description, I encoded parts of it into a computational problem solving model and demonstrated that the computational model produces behaviours similar to the behaviours of students. I also triangulated the descriptions against written tests and interviews, showing that distinctions in the descriptions correlate with differential performances on the tests, and with students' explanations in interviews. This methodology and a comprehensive overview of results are described in detail elsewhere (Roschelle, 1991). Detailed case studies from this research appear in several publications (e.g., Roschelle & Clancey, 1992; Roschelle, 1992b; Teasley & Roschelle, 1993). In this chapter, I draw examples from these studies that exemplify the rationale for shifting from an epistemic fidelity to a mediated collaborative inquiry point of view. I present these as a series of lessons learned.

> LESSON ONE: Embodying a mental model in a physical object always introduces unwanted features. Internal contradictions of high fidelity design are ordinarily resolved by adopting arbitrary conventions, creating the problem for the newcomer of separating conventional from referential display features.

Some physicists who saw EM argued that it had low epistemic fidelity because acceleration appears at the tip of velocity rather than at the base of the particle. They suggested that this encourages the interpretation that acceleration acts at a distance, not on the object. This argument is a case of conflicting interpretation of the high fidelity principle: the EM representation is high fidelity in terms of the relationships among position, velocity and acceleration, but not in terms of the locality of action. In truth, the position of the acceleration is arbitrary and meaningless; only its displacement matters.

Empirically, I found no evidence in my research that students saw acceleration acting at a distance (Roschelle, 1991). Moreover, informal experiments demonstrated that the conventional representation, which draws both velocity and acceleration from the center of the particle, can be quite problematic. Students see it as indicating that acceleration and velocity are equal-and-opposite when coming to a stop (this is a misconception). Moreover, students often try to interpret a line connecting the two arrow tips as the result, rather than first shifting the position of the acceleration. (Learners can construct problematic interpretations for any external representation.)

Furthermore, in this case a contradiction occurs because there is no physical way to represent a displacement vector without putting it somewhere. There is always the potential for someone to interpret the placement as meaningful. Such arbitrary decisions plague the designer of physical representations for mathematical and conceptual objects, because these are often dimensionless or infinite (thus either invisible or impossible to fit into finite space).

> LESSON TWO: Newcomers often did not use the EM appropriately, did not recognise the critical aspects of the display, or did not focus their attention the way a physicist would. The very features of the display that correspond to an expert mental model were often invisible to students.

For example, most students did not pay attention to the change in the velocity vector over time. Instead, they watched the circle that represents the particle. On many occasions, the experimenter told the students that it would be helpful in understanding the display to look at the moving vector. This advice was ignored: Students did not look at the changing velocity until they developed an idea spontaneously that made it worthwhile to look.

Conversely, students were fascinated by artefacts of the display. For instance, when the particle goes slowly the trace dots smudge together to form a line segment. Students wanted to identify the precise difference between distinct dots and a line-smudge. From the expert point of view, this is an unwanted artefact of the limited pixel density of the computer display. Experts readily ignore the smudges.

When students did notice relevant features, their choice of labels was sometimes problematic (Roschelle, 1991). For example, Jack and Ken understood the first few trace dots as measuring an objects' acceleration. These dots are in fact a better measure of initial speed. Carol and Dana got hung up by looking at *distance* and calling it *speed*. More generally, students labelled speeds with positive amounts only. This led to difficulties in their explanations. Whereas a scientist using all the real numbers (positive and negative) can describe gravitational acceleration as uniformly decreasing velocity, students using only positive numbers had to account for a sudden switch from decreasing to increasing speed.

Also, unlike scientists, students often did not know what to do in order to learn from this display. For example, students would often make EM motions that were as fast as possible; science educators made relatively slow motions. Of course, it was quite difficult for the newcomers to make good observations of very fast motions. Likewise, students often chose inappropriate settings of velocity and acceleration. For example, they would make initial velocity very small relative to acceleration. In this situation, the effect of initial velocity is negligible, leading newcomers to the incorrect hypothesis that initial velocity doesn't matter.

Finally, even when students labelled features appropriately, they often selected the wrong combinations of features for the highest levels of attention. Carol and Dana, for example, focussed on *setting* initial velocity but on *observing* average speed. In the parabola, they got confused by focussing on its height, width, and the total trip time, rather than focussing on initial velocity and change in velocity. Quera and Randi went astray by focussing on the position of acceleration, not on its direction and length. In particular, they described the acceleration vector as being attracted to a certain place, and dragged the velocity and the particle along with it. Only when the acceleration reached its place of attraction did the length and direction of acceleration have import, in Quera's account.

> LESSON THREE: Despite a high fidelity representation, students construct mental models in a form that seems useful and natural from *their* world view. Thus, their constructed knowledge can be different *in kind* from the target knowledge, while still enabling them to succeed at the given task.

A third class of failures has to do with students' sense of mechanism, observed in the form of a bias toward certain forms of knowledge and explanation. Students often are predisposed to first-order mechanisms -- mechanisms in which each controllable parameter directly relates to an outcome variable. In contrast, acceleration is a second-order concept; effects of acceleration on motion are seen through an intermediate variable, velocity. Nonetheless, students constructed mental models of the EM display in which acceleration was first-order. A common model was to map the velocity vector onto the initial motion, and speed and acceleration onto the latter direction and speed (Roschelle, 1991).

Through video tape analysis, I identified three forms of knowledge that students constructed in order to solve EM problems and to explain their work. One might expect that because the EM is based on the definition of acceleration, students who succeed on the task would formulate something close to the definition of acceleration (acceleration is change in velocity over time). This was not the case. Students only rarely generated compact definitions, and then only at the very end of their experience with the EM. More commonly, they constructed knowledge using elements of three forms: registrations (features noticed and attended to), qualitative cases, and metaphoric abstractions (Roschelle, 1991).

A qualitative case is a group of qualitative regularities that apply within a particular kind of motion. Within each case, students constructed knowledge of many regularities. For example, within the case of a vertical ball toss:

HEIGHT IS PROPORTIONAL

TO THE LENGTH OF VELOCITY

Qualitative case knowledge has the character of a loose aggregate, without any necessary internal consistency or coherence. To generate coherence, students bring metaphoric abstractions to bear. For example, students commonly explain the relationship between acceleration and velocity as a "pull." The acceleration pulls the tip of velocity, changing its length and direction. Such metaphors can unite the elements of a case, and can span cases, as described in the scientific philosophy of Max Black (Black, 1979; 1962).

Roschelle (1991) presents much detailed evidence about the nature of the qualitative cases and metaphor abstractions constructed by students as they use the EM. Herein, I shall simply state an important generalisation: Students' knowledge is different *in kind* from the knowledge attributed to the expert mental model. In particular, student knowledge is composed of relations among many fragmentary qualitative cases and metaphoric abstractions, whereas physicists link every element of their mental model to a single abstract mathematical definition.

Furthermore, the specific pieces of knowledge that students construct are often problematic from the scientific point of view. For example, students often construct a regularity that links the "width" of a parabola to the angle between velocity and acceleration. Scientists don't think in terms of widths of parabolas and angles between vectors. Students often choose knowledge elements that express relationships between the initial configuration and the global form of a trajectory (e.g., bigger velocity in a toss makes total trip time longer). Scientists prefer local relationships (e.g., bigger velocity means more distance per each unit of time), from which they derive global regularities. Finally, students have little interest in compact, consistent forms of knowledge; they often seem perfectly happy to construct many little pieces of knowledge which they adapt ad hoc to solve particular challenges.

It seems quite unlikely that these problems could be overcome by strong epistemic fidelity. A better picture of the expert mental model is unlikely to encourage students to construct mathematical definitions instead of qualitative cases and abstract metaphors. Moreover, a better picture is unlikely to change students' preferences for global instead of local regularities and for fragmentary, adaptable knowledge over compact and consistent knowledge.

More precisely, many of the "constraints" in the expert mental model reside not in knowledge, but in the culture of representational practice to which the expert belongs. Students construct a model based on their experience and the constraints of their own community. Because a designer cannot reduce practice to theory (Clancey, 1992), we cannot fully embody a culture-specific reasoning practice in an artefact.

LESSON FOUR: Major transformations in a mental model occur when students encounter a problematic experience. Problematic experiences are hard to predict based on a description of an experts' mental model, though they do occur with regularity under conditions that can be described if one understands how students think.

The empirical data show an overall pattern in students' learning with the EM. As students encounter the EM initially, they engage in a form of routine coping. The knowledge they construct in this first phase bears little similarity to scientific knowledge, though it is sufficient for solving most tasks. At some point, usually after about one hour, students' experiences become problematic: They become frustrated and confused. The device no longer presents a clear course of action, their loose assemblage of pieces of knowledge oscillates wildly between incompatible points of view, and they experience a genuine breakdown in their capability to cope with the EM. In their attempts to resolve these problematic experiences, students can transform their mental models dramatically, bringing them considerably closer to an expert model.

Surprisingly, some of the most problematic aspects for students are the least problematic elements from the point of view of an expert mental model.

An example involves students' descriptions of stopped motions. From the expert point of view, this is trivial: Velocity is zero. Students, on the other hand, (a) fail to distinguish between an instantaneous and an extended stop and (b) expect forces at stop to "balance" (i.e., be equal and opposite). As a result, they are intensely frustrated and puzzled when the EM depicts a constant acceleration even when velocity is zero at the top of the vertical ball toss. From their first-order perspective, the presence of a "force" requires the presence of motion. As it turns out, a correct understanding of how to describe "stopped" motion is the last aspect of the EM that students come to conceive of in scientific terms.

The second circumstance that generates a problematic experience for students is the parabola. They expect velocity to be aligned with the beginning of the motion and acceleration to be symmetrically aligned with the end of the motion. That is, students expect a parabola to be the result of conjoining two first-order parameters, one for the beginning of the motion and one for the end. When this fails to work, they make acceleration longer and longer, in order to make its effect in ending the motion more prominent. This makes the shape of the parabola less and less symmetric, so they then make the parabola smaller and smaller. After a while, they get intensely frustrated because no settings of acceleration seem to produce a symmetrical parabola. As they get frustrated, they experiment with more varied settings of acceleration. Sooner or later, they set acceleration to point straight down. To their great surprise, this produces a symmetrical parabola.

But this makes no sense to students. They expect that a downward acceleration should produce a motion, with its latter half travelling straight down. The conflict they experience becomes the occasion for a process of inquiry which seeks to transform their mental model -- to make it more coherent and unified. The result of this inquiry can be a mental model in which acceleration is a second-order parameter (a result documented in several case studies).

Thus, a detailed understanding of an expert's mental model will not tell us when and how students learn: One would not expect the "stopping" to be prominent or articulated in detail in an expert mental model. Nor would it be obvious that parabolic motion produces a conflict within students' first-order world view. Epistemic fidelity therefore cannot focus the designers' attention on the aspects of the display that will most likely trigger and support learning.

These lessons attack the basic assumptions of the epistemic fidelity design perspective. Recall the definition of epistemic fidelity, in terms of a correspondence between a physical representation and an abstract, ideal mental model. Under an internalisation theory of learning, this correspondence should enable students to see and internalise the mental model. To the contrary, however, video tape analysis of students' learning showed that the correspondence was only visible to people who already understood the subject matter. Students often did not distinguish arbitrary from meaningful design elements, did not recognise the critical aspects of the display, and did not choose to make sense of the display in the way a physicist would. Furthermore, the conditions under which students learned could not be predicted purely from an analysis of the expert's model. In summary, high fidelity design is not a guarantee of better learning outcomes.

4. Lessons about mediating collaborative inquiry

Despite the problems outlined above, the empirical evidence shows that the EM can help students learn. EM is one variant in a long sequence of Newtonian computer simulations including Dynaturtle (diSessa, 1982) and ThinkerTools (White, 1993). Extensive studies show that these computer microworlds are among the most powerful techniques for helping students learn (e.g., White, 1993). My own video studies show that students who use the EM often change their concepts dramatically in ways that make their descriptions of motion much more compatible with Newtonian theory (Roschelle, 1991).

Thus, in this chapter a crucial distinction is made between the propositions that (a) computer visualisation tools can help students learn and that (b) students learn because computer visualisation tools are designed according the principle of epistemic fidelity. In the previous section, I showed that students do not learn because the visual model embodies an expert mental model; such correspondences are rendered invisible from within a students' world view. My concern in this section is to articulate (a) positive principles that describe the nature of student learning, and (b) how tools can be designed to enable more students to be successful.

Barbara White's work provides a good example. White (1993) has performed extensive experiments with a similar tool called ThinkerTools. White has shown that 6th grade students can attain conceptual understanding of velocity and acceleration that surpasses that of 12th grade students, by using ThinkerTools.

Three differences distinguish White's work from an epistemic fidelity design approach.

First, White developed ThinkerTools to support students' inquiry process as they encountered the problem of describing frictionless motion. No pretensions are made that ThinkerTools corresponds to representations in an expert's mental model. Indeed, White has not studied physicists' mental imagery; images that appear on the ThinkerTools screen are not plausible images in an experts' mental model. White's design supports the ways in which students actually build knowledge, rather than assuming a process of internalisation via an explicit expert model. The fidelity incorporated in ThinkerTools is computational, not representational -- ThinkerTools computes motion the way a physicist would, though it doesn't necessarily portray it with expert mental representations.

Second, White embeds students' use of ThinkerTools within a curriculum that teaches explicitly about the nature of scientific law and the process of scientific inquiry. Thus, White is giving students specific ideas and processes to think with -- not just "embodied models".

Third, White assigns a strong priority to discussion among students and between the teacher and students. By structuring these conversations in the image of scientific discussions, White creates a social climate (context) which further constrains the process of constructing and verifying knowledge.

Research with the Envisioning Machine has focused on understanding the process by which students construct knowledge, and the relation of that process to design. I give a capsule summary of students' learning process here, then discuss four design principles within a mediated collaborative inquiry process. The empirical details supporting this description of the learning process are found in Roschelle (1991).

Students who use the EM construct a mental model. At first, the mental models they form have little correlation with expert mental models. They register different features of the display than an expert does. They formulate different qualitative regularities than an expert would (e.g., the angle between velocity and acceleration is proportional to the width of the parabola), and they use metaphors (e.g., pulling, hinging, adding) where the expert mental model uses definitions.

Over time, however, students can transform their mental models into closer approximations of scientists' mental models. The process by which this occurs is best described as "inquiry", in the sense meant by Dewey (1938, p. 104):

> the controlled or directed transformation of an indeterminate situation into one that is so determinate in its constituent distinctions and relations as to convert the elements of the original situation into a unified whole.

Dewey's notion of inquiry flowed from his conception of a problematic experience (Dewey, 1938). He brought to attention the fact that we often experience life as routine coping with familiar situations. Some situations, however, are problematic. By this, Dewey means that the situation is confusing, unsettled, disturbing, and most importantly, lacking clear possibilities for action.

By "inquiry", Dewey means a practical activity that transforms the situation into one that is more clearly articulated, unified, and comprehensible -- and in which the directions for successful action are now clear. Importantly, this process involves uncovering previously unnoticed features of the situation and constructing new relationships that tie them together. Inquiry is a productive and constructive craft. Moreover, Dewey believes successful inquiries have objective results: Inquiry produces real changes in the coupling of the person and the situation with which he or she is engaged. This change is located neither in the person nor in the situation, but in interaction between person and situation (both physical and social).

Dewey's definition of inquiry refers not just to problematic experience, but also (equally) to the tools and practices that enable gradual transformation into a resolved, determinate situation. Clearly, an educative experience can only be successful if it both engages students in a problematic situation and provides suitable tools for the transformation of that situation. In the remainder of this section, I discuss design principles (in the form of further lessons) that describe the nature of such tools.

Before doing so, one thing must be made clear: The situations in which students successfully engage in inquiry are *both* social and cognitive. Students who successfully learn with the EM or ThinkerTools (White, 1993) do so both because of their relationships both to physical tools and to other students and teachers. Inquiry, in Dewey's sense (and in the sense it is used here), is a communicative, collaborative practice.

Much has been written about the benefits of collaborative learning and of the set of trade-offs involved in assigning students to teams (e.g., Johnson & Johnson, 1987; Slavin, 1990). Collaboration appears to enhance learning by providing a context in which students are more likely to construct, elaborate and critique explanations (Hooper, 1992). The empirical case studies that substantiate this point with respect to the EM can be found particularly in Roschelle (1992), Roschelle & Clancey (1992), and Teasley & Roschelle (1993).

Collaboratively constructing shared explanations is not always easy, and is often troublesome. The lessons that follow highlight some of the problems that commonly arise in collaborative inquiry and present design guidelines that enable students to overcome these problems. Rather than orienting the designer to better ways of representing knowledge (as in epistemic fidelity), these principles focus on supporting communicative practices that enable students to collaboratively construct, elaborate and critique explanations.

> LESSON FIVE: Design displays that will extend students' engagement with problematic situations, and provide repeated access to the same problems. This will enable students to come to see different things each time a problem is accessed, and give them time to talk about a problematic experience before it disappears.

One function of technology in inquiry is to provide stable, long-term access to a problematic situation that may occur infrequently or may be short-lived. In the EM situation, motions occur in real-time. Thus, the aspects of a motion that are problematic to students may occur fleetingly. This impedes collaboration, because students find it hard to share an explanation when they cannot share sustained access to the puzzling phenomena.

As a consequence, one subtle but highly effective adjustment was made in the EM. In previous designs, the RESET command both moved the particle back to its initial position and erased the dots produced by the previous motion. The problem with this method was that students had to reset in order to make adjustments to vectors, but having reset they could no longer refer to the previous motion (in order to justify their adjustments). Thus, a student could not explain a change to his or her partner. In the final version of the EM, the dots are erased at the onset of the PLAY command; they are left on the screen to support conversations about the previous motion while adjustments to the vectors for the next motion are being made.

Likewise, because speed is a focal concept in students' inquiries, the EM provides a way to extend students' engagement with the experience of speed. Speed is redundantly represented in the trace dots, the length of the velocity vector, and the simulated speed of the particle across the screen. This selective use of redundancy pairs the ephemeral, but easily-interpreted representation of speed as simulated motion with the more persistent representation of speed as trace dot spacing. Interestingly, as students become experts with the EM, they tend to watch the trace dots as the primary representation, viewing the running simulation as redundant, occasionally useful information.

It is not clear that expert mental models would have these features. When do the dots get erased in the expert's head? Who knows if experts even see dots in their mental model? How many redundant representations of speed appear in the experts' mental models? These questions may not be answerable. On the other hand, it is obvious from the video tape evidence that students' process of collaborative inquiry requires the persistence of the dots on the screen, the ability to repeat a segment of motion, and the redundancy of representations. These features enable students to collaborate by allowing them to share sustained access to particular problematic situations over a long period of time.

LESSON SIX: Support selective attention to parts, and attention to the connections between parts and wholes. Provide tools for participants to establish a shared focus of attention and to trace connections from their local focus of attention to the overall context.

Another impediment to collaboration is that individual students often focus on different elements of a phenomenon, or explain things relative to different contexts. Thus, another function of technology in collaborative inquiry is to provide a way of focusing attention on specific attributes, while nonetheless retaining the connection of those attributes to the broader context of the problematic situation.

For example, Roschelle & Clancey (1992) examine a case where two students collaboratively build an understanding of acceleration. This occurs through a process whereby students coordinate individual insights, to construct shared meanings. At one point in the collaboration, Gerry generates an insight about how parabolic motion is produced. Hal asks for and receives an explanation, but indicates that he cannot make sense of it. As the case unfolds, it turns out that Hal cannot understand Gerry's explanation because he is not attending to the features of the EM display that support the explanation.

Eventually, Hal and Gerry are able to build a shared understanding. Many features of the EM enable these students to overcome the lack of a shared focus of attention that is blocking their ability to communicate. Herein, I shall mention just two such features.

First, whereas early versions of the EM played a continuous motion, later versions allow students to step through a motion one second at a time. Gerry explicitly chooses to use this feature to focus Hal's attention. He runs the simulation forward one second, and then describes the difference he is attending to -- a change in the velocity arrow. Hal begins to focus on this object. The step by step motion slows the simulation to make it easier for students to synchronise their conversation with the simulation, and thereby to communicate about the objects they are registering.

Second, the EM portrays vectors that are approximately the same length as a human finger. Gerry uses this affordance to communicate what he is seeing to Hal: he overlays his finger on top of the vector and imitates its behaviour. This helps Hal pick this feature out of the visual field as a discrete object.

Similarly, students often use the trace dots as a way to make distinctions between instantaneous and average speed. At first, this distinction is very hard for students to make and to apply. However, by pointing either at a local segment of trace dots or at dots representing the distance travelled in a set time, students can achieve a focus either on local speed or on overall speed. Importantly, these distinctions are made via communicative practices. In order to explain their ideas to someone else, students point to

aspects of the screen that can provide a set of features visible to all parties.

In a truly mental model, focus of attention should not be a problem. Experts would only include in their mental model those features which are important to them. Thus, the principle of epistemic fidelity is of little help in deciding how to help learners focus their attention -- especially when they may not even notice those features that experts consider essential. The lesson of focus and context directs a designer's attention to creating displays that enable collaborators to achieve a common focus of attention and to connect their local conversation to a larger context.

LESSON SEVEN: Enable communicative action. Support communication through action, and match visualisations to the language that students have available to describe the visualisations.

Expert physicists have a language ready-at-hand in which to describe their mental models. Students do not. For example, students' language does not contain suitable distinctions between average and instantaneous speed. Nor do students use mathematic constructs (e.g., "a derivative") readily as a basis for formulating their ideas. In addition, many students have trouble expressing their conceptions through language at all. They fall back on gesture as an alternative mode of communication (Crowder & Newman, 1993). Thus, the ability to talk about a mental model depends upon the community of practice to which a person belongs.

This point applies to many of the design decisions that make the EM a success. For example, many students communicate "an idea" to another student by making an adjustment to the vectors. But early on it became apparent that students were having trouble tracking the changes made by their partners.

Two specific changes to the design were made. First, the vectors were constrained to a grid. As they were adjusted to each new grid setting, an audible click occurred. Second, as a vector was dragged the previous vector was left visible on the screen (so that students could observe easily the difference between the previous and current settings). These changes enable participants to interpret the communicative intent of their partner's actions more clearly. Specifically, while using the EM students often negotiate qualitative cases through action: One student might say "it's too fast", while the other student makes the velocity arrow shorter (Teasley & Roschelle, 1993). This communicates a qualitative regularity between length of velocity and speed.

Similarly, the EM was explicitly designed to enable students to use the metaphor of "pulling" to describe the relationship between velocity and acceleration. The metaphor of pulling can enable students to make sense of acceleration as a property that changes the length and direction of velocity simultaneously -- they see the acceleration vector pulling the tip of the velocity vector to a new location in velocity space. When students lack the concept of a derivative, they can use pulling as a qualitative approximation of the idea. And although pulling is not the same concept as a derivative, through combination with other metaphors and gradual refinement students can generate an abstract concept that is quite similar to the derivative concept. Thus, while placement of the acceleration arrow in the EM is unconventional and does not correspond to an expert's mental model, this placement does make it easier for students to communicate about a critical concept.

> LESSON EIGHT: One should design activities which engage students actively in doing, and in encountering meaningful experiential feedback as a consequence of their actions.

A defining feature of interactive learning environments is that they offer students an opportunity for learning by doing. Learning by doing, however, means many things to many people. The EM design closely follows an explicit specification of learning by doing: Dewey's account of inquiry. Inquiry is a cycle of four stages, as depicted in Figure 3.

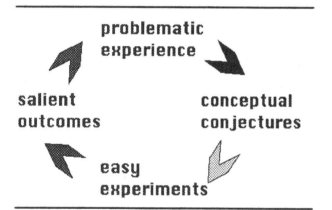

Figure 3. Dewey's cycle of inquiry

Lesson 5 discussed how the EM is designed to ensure that students encounter situations that are problematic (from their point of view). Although it is important that students experience a problem fully as their own, it would be a mistake for them to dwell too long in this problematic state. Hence, it is important that this stage quickly give rise to conceptual conjectures.

The design of the EM uses objects which are highly suggestive of conceptual meanings. For example, arrows readily evoke direction and force, as well as related concepts like pulling and guiding. Moreover, students can make things bigger or smaller easily, and align directions. Thus, when they encounter a problem students quickly generate conceptual conjecture.

The conceptual conjecture phase must give way to easy experimentation. Since students' problems are encountered as experiences, they must be resolved in experiences. Therefore, it is important that the EM uses direct

manipulation techniques to enable students to carry out experiments quickly according to their conjectures. This is easy if they can adjust a vector with the mouse, then re-run the simulation. Ease of experimentation encourages students to subject their concepts to the test of experience.

Experimentation, however, would not be useful if outcomes were obscure. Herein lies a subtle but crucial feature of the EM design: it gives students a very simple, perceptual criterion to determine success. Motions must be "the same." Interestingly, students' operationalisations of "the same" evolves as they use the simulation. Many students begin by simply making motions that go in the same direction. Once this is achieved, their eyes tell them that speeds need to be the same, too. In adjusting speeds, they find that they cannot make motions "the same" unless they address changes in speed as well. Finally, as students progress, they start to change from a simple perceptual judgement of "the same" to a more instrumental judgement (e.g., making measurements using features such as trace dots). Importantly, students can make all these judgements without external authority. The EM gives students a criterion for success that they can interpret and use readily.

5. Conclusion

Suchman (1987, p. 69), in her analysis of planning and situated action, articulates a point that resonates with our observations of students' learning while using the EM:

> For students of purposeful action, however, the observation that action interpretation is inherently uncertain does have a methodological consequence: Namely, it recommends that we turn our attention from explaining away uncertainty in the interpretation of action to identifying the resources by which the inevitable uncertainty is managed.

As was apparent in research on students' use of the EM, "inevitable uncertainty" applies not only to interpretation of actions, but also to interpretation of displays. Designers of high fidelity displays try to eliminate this uncertainty by perfecting the denotational relationship between a display and the ideal form of the underlying concepts. Unfortunately, gaps in world views usually prevent learners from decoding the denotational relationship and acquiring the target understanding. Hence, rather than merely representing mental models accurately, designers must focus on supporting communicative practices that enable ambiguities and uncertainties to be resolved smoothly. Designers must provide a medium that facilitates collaborative inquiry.

Displays with high epistemic fidelity are not necessarily the best for negotiating the meaning of a conversation (Roschelle & Clancey, 1992) or for demonstrating a concept (diSessa, 1986). A simple example is the fact that the

EM simulation is stopped while the student adjusts velocity and acceleration. Strictly speaking, this does not make sense: If an object has a non-zero velocity, it is moving. Time cannot be "frozen." Conversely, properties that violate high fidelity often make for good conversations. For example, discrete numerical simulations often introduce an accumulating error as the simulation progresses. Noticing this error can stimulate a conversation about the difference between a theory and a numerical simulation. The Alternate Reality Kit (Smith, 1986) takes this approach to the extreme, purposely displaying interactive worlds that violate scientific laws in order to stimulate an understanding of the laws of our world. Thus, the lack of high fidelity can create the background for a discussion of serious scientific issues.

Another concern is the presence of internal conflicts in the application of epistemic fidelity. In the EM, such internal conflicts occurred when ideal mathematical objects such as the acceleration displacement vector were given concrete representations and thus came to embody unintentional, low-fidelity properties. Similar conflicts occurred when continuous motion was (necessarily) modelled by numerical simulation in finite time steps, with finite size points. Concrete or reified representations (which are often thought to be the best for learning) are especially prone to introducing unwanted properties, and thus reducing epistemic fidelity. These concerns with epistemic fidelity are evidenced by data from video analysis of the EM. It was observed that students do not interpret displays as intended despite the high fidelity of the representation, from an expert's point of view.

Thus, it is important to make a distinction among the ways of applying the mental model concept to computer system design. On one hand, it is essential that students have a good mental model of how the computer system works (Norman, 1991). Thus, students control the EM using commands named PLAY, FORWARD, and BACKWARD. This tape recorder model makes it easy for students to run the simulation. On the other hand, educators who design software sometimes attempt to map a conceptual mental model to a set of computational objects. This is a generalisation from (a) learning how to control a computer system to (b) learning how to control a computer system in order to understand the system of concepts it denotes (or represents). Such generalisation does not work across the boundaries of world views: Problems of knowing what to do, where to look, and how to make sense diminish the possibility of the student seeing the intended epistemic correspondence.

To summarise, while it is generally true that designing a good mental model will help users control a computer system, representing knowledge in a computational model does not necessarily help students construct the intended knowledge. Designing a medium that supports communicative practices and constructive learning processes is at least as important as representing knowledge with fidelity.

Epistemic fidelity and mediated collaborative inquiry perspectives also suggest different design methodologies. Epistemic fidelity lends itself to top-down specification: Researchers can study an expert model and use it as a specification for the interface to be designed. Mediating collaborative inquiry suggests an iterative process incorporating such ideas as participatory design (Greenbaum & Kyng, 1991), collaborative rapid prototyping (Bodker & Gronbaek, 1991), and video interaction analysis (Suchman & Trigg, 1991). Describing these techniques fully is outside the scope of the this chapter.

Iteration and rapid prototyping correctly suggest a strong trial and error component of the process. However, these methods are not merely trial and error. Participatory design, collaborative prototyping, and video interaction analysis are powerful techniques for identifying communicative practices that enable collaborative learning. The lessons I have described suggest ways of selectively emphasising experimentation so as to focus design energies on producing a medium that empowers conversational and learning processes, rather than merely increasing the fidelity of knowledge representations to mental models. While trial and error is part of any designer's repertoire, a design perspective strongly influences the outcome by determining what factors are considered or ignored. All too often, communicative practice and learning process have been ignored in favour of knowledge representation.

Are the epistemic fidelity and mediated collaborative inquiry perspectives incompatible? It is an essential feature of the EM (and other similar simulations) that they compute motions in accordance with a Newtonian world view. Faithful computational fidelity to Newton's perspective is a prerequisite for success. Computational fidelity, however, is a considerably weaker constraint than epistemic fidelity: It specifies computational relationships between successive states in the simulation, but not interpretative or epistemic relationships between different forms of imagery. The empirical data do not bear out the view that students directly profit from the higher level of epistemic correspondence; experts see the correspondence, but learners from a different world view do not.

In addition to computational fidelity, I have argued that learning technologies should be designed to support the social process of inquiry through which students learn. Mental models are constituted not just by theoretical knowledge, but also by a range of practices that cannot be encoded in observer-independent form. Thus, an external model cannot encode a target mental model into a "conduit" such that a student coming from another world view can readily decode it.

External models, however, can support communicative practices, and conversations across world views are possible under the right circumstances. The necessary affordances for inquiry and collaboration include extended engagement with problematic experiences, establishment of selective attention to parts and wholes, support for communicative action, and an activity that makes sense within both world views. By supporting communicative practices that seek to overcome ambiguities and uncertainties in meaning, designers can enable conversations in which participants gradually learn to participate in the expert world view.

Acknowledgments

This chapter draws upon material presented at a Symposium on Knowledge-Based Environments for Learning and Teaching, Stanford, CA, March 1990, and at AERA Symposium on Dynamic Diagrams for Model-Based Science Learning, April, 1990. Portions of this chapter have circulated as a draft manuscript under the title "Designing for Conversations." I thank the many colleagues at the Institute for Research on Learning, Stanford, and UC Berkeley who have commented on earlier versions of this chapter.

References

BLACK, M. 1979, More about metaphor, in A. Ortony (ed), *Metaphor and Thought* (Cambridge University Press, Cambridge, England), 19-43.

BLACK, M. 1962, *Models and Metaphors* (Cornell University Press, Ithaca, NY).

BODKER, S. & GRONBAEK, K. 1991, Cooperative prototyping: users and designers in mutual activity, in J. Greenbaum & M. Kyng (eds), *Design at Work: Cooperative Design of Computer Systems* (Lawrence Erlbaum, Hillsdale, NJ).

BOULDING, K. 1985, *Human Betterment* (Sage Publications, Beverly Hills, CA).

CARRAMAZZA, A., McCLOSKEY, M., & GREEN, B. 1981, Naive beliefs in "sophisticated" subjects: misconceptions about trajectories of objects. *Cognition* 9, 117-123.

CLANCEY, W.J. 1989, The frame of reference problem in the design of intelligent machines, in K. van Lehn & A. Newall (eds), *Architectures for Intelligence* (Lawrence Erlbaum, Hillsdale, NJ).

CLANCEY, W.J 1992, Practice Cannot Be Reduced to Theory: Knowledge Representation and Change in the Workplace. Presentation at the NATO Workshop on Organizational Change, Siena, Italy, September 22-26, 1992. To appear in S. Bagnara, C. Zuccermaglio, S. Stucky (eds), *Organizational Learning and Technological Change* (Springer-Verlag, Berlin).

CROWDER, E.M. & NEWMAN, D. 1993, Telling what they know: the role of gesture and language in children's science explanations. *Pragmatics & Cognition* 1 (2), 339-374.

DEWEY, J. 1938, *Logic: The Theory of Inquiry* (Henry Holt, New York).

DISESSA, A.A. 1986, Artificial worlds and real experience, *Instructional Science* 14, 207-227.

DISESSA, A.A. 1982, Unlearning Aristotelean physics: a study of knowledge-based learning. *Cognitive Science* 6.

GENTNER, D. & STEVENS, A.L. (Eds.) *Mental Models* (Lawrence Erlbaum, Hillsdale, NJ).

GREENBAUM, J. & KYNG, M. 1991, *Design at Work: Cooperative Design of Computer Systems* (Lawrence Erlbaum, Hillsdale, NJ).

HALHOUN, I.A. & HESTENES, D. 1985, The initial knowledge state of college physics students. *American Journal of Physics* 53, 1056-1065.

HOOPER, S. 1992, Cooperative learning and computer-based instruction. *Education Technology Research and Development* 40 (3), 21-38.

JIH. H.J., & REEVES, T.C. 1992, Mental models: a research focus for interative learning systems. *Education Technology Research & Development* 40 (3), 39-53.

JOHNSON, D.W. & JOHNSON, R.T. 1987, *Learning Together and Alone* (Prentice Hall, Englewood Cliffs, NJ).

JOHNSON-LAIRD, P.N. 1983, *Mental Models* (Cambridge University Press, Cambridge, England).

KIERAS, D.E. & BOVAIR, S. 1984, The role of a mental model in learning to operate a device. *Cognitive Science* 8 (3), 255-273.

LAVE, J. & WENGER, E. 1989, Situated learning: legitimate Peripheral Participation (Report No. IRL-89-0013). Institute for Research on Learning, Palo Alto, CA.

McDERMOTT, L.C. 1984, Research on conceptual understanding in mechanics. *Physics Today* 37, 24-32.

NEWMAN, D., GRIFFITH, P., & COLE, M. 1989, *The Construction Zone: Working for Cognitive Change in School* (Cambridge University Press, Cambridge, England).

NORMAN, D.A. 1991, *The Psychology of Everyday Things* (Basic Books, New York).

REDDY, M. 1979, The conduit metaphor: a case of frame conflict in our language about language, in A. Ortony (ed), *Metaphor and Thought* (Cambridge University Press, Cambridge, England).

ROSCHELLE, J. 1992a, Mediated collaborative inquiry: towards a practical philosophy of learning technology, in M. Ryan (ed), *Classrooms: Where Ideas Meet Reality*, (Queensland Society for Information Technology in Education, Brisbane, Australia).

ROSCHELLE, J. 1992b, Learning by collaborating: convergent conceptual change. *Journal of the Learning Sciences* 2, 235-276.

ROSCHELLE, J. 1991, Students' Construction of Qualitative Physics Knowledge: learning About Velocity and Acceleration in a Computer Microworld. Doctoral dissertation, University of California, Berkeley (unpublished).

ROSCHELLE, J. AND CLANCEY, W.J. 1992, Learning as social and neural. *Educational Psychologist* 27, 435-453.

ROSCHELLE, J. AND GREENO, J., 1987, Mental Models in Expert Physics Problem Solving, ONR Report GK-2. Available from School of Education, University of California, Berkeley, CA.

SLAVIN, R.E. 1990, *Cooperative Learning: Theory, Research, and Practice* (Prentice Hall, Englewood Cliffs, NJ).

SUCHMAN, L. 1987, *Plans and Situated Action* (Cambridge University Press, New York).

SUCHMAN, L. & TRIGG, R. 1991, Understanding practice: video as a medium for reflection and design, in J. Greenbaum & M. Kyng (eds), *Design at Work: Cooperative Design of Computer Systems* (Lawrence Erlbaum, Hillsdale, NJ).

SMITH, D.C., IRBY, C., KIMBALL, R., & VERPLANK, W.L. 1982, Designing the Star user interface. *Byte* 7 (4).

SMITH, R.B. 1986, The Alternate Reality Kit: An Animated Environment for Creating Interactive Simulations. Paper presented to the IEEE Computer Society Workshop on Visual Languages, Dallas, Texas, June 26, 1986.

TAUBERMANN, M.J. & ACKERMANN, D. (eds). 1990, *Mental Models and Human Computer Interaction 1* (Elsevier, Amsterdam).

TAUBERMANN, M.J. & ACKERMANN, D. (eds). 1991, *Mental Models and Human Computer Interaction 2* (Elsevier, Amsterdam).

TEASLEY, S.D. AND ROSCHELLE, J. 1993, Constructing a Joint Problem Space: the computer as a tool for sharing knowledge,in S.P. Lajoie & S.J. Derry (eds), *The Computer As A Cognitive Tool* (Lawrence Erlbaum, Hillsdale, NJ), 229-258.

WENGER, E. 1987, *Artificial Intelligence and Tutoring Systems* (Morgan Kaufmann, Los Altos, CA).

WHITE, B.Y. 1993, ThinkerTools: causal models, conceptual change, and science education. *Cognition and Instruction* **10** (1), 1-100.

VYGOTSKY, L.S. 1978, Mind in society: the development of higher psychological processes. M. Cole, V. John-Steiner, S. Scribner, & E. Souberman (eds), (Harvard University Press, Cambridge, MA).

YOUNG, R.M. 1981, The machine inside the machine: users' models of pocket calculators. *International Journal of Man-Machine Studies* **15**, 87-134.

3

Computer-mediated interpersonal communication: the HCHI approach

LAJOS BALINT

Dept. of Natural Sciences, Hungarian Academy of Sciences, Budapest, Nador-U.7., H-1051, Hungary
h48bal@ella.hu

Abstract. This chapter investigates general aspects and basic concepts of computer-aided human-to-human interaction, and suggests a new method of using specific computerised tools in the support of human communications.

The key concept in the HCHI (human-computer-human interaction) approach is the introduction of specific, intentional computer-based processing of human messages, in which an intelligent machine aids human-to-human information transfer. The machine supports not only acquisition, storage, sorting, merging and retrieval of transmitted information, but also translation, formalisation, re-recording, analysis and re-synthesising of human-to-human messages. Moreover, filtering, adjusting, correcting and extracting key facts is possible, as is the constrained transfer of related mental models, via suitable decoding/encoding of messages. All of these properties result in enhanced precision and increased reliability in human-to-human information transfer -- especially in complex man-machine systems.

1. Introduction

Theoretical and practical questions of human-computer interaction have been at the focus of research and development devoted to man-machine systems (MMS) for many years (Helander, 1988; Rasmussen, 1991). Related activities have sought to achieve effective and reliable communication between humans and machines.

However, it is rarely emphasised that the widely accepted need of investigating methods of human-computer interaction should be complemented by similarly intensive investigations with respect to human-to-human interaction (HHI) -- which encompasses a wide variety of unanswered questions, both in theory and practice (Bayley, 1982; Vickers, 1989).

No satisfactory effort has been devoted to increasing the efficiency and reliability of human-to-human interaction in complex man-machine systems. This communication domain is sometimes more ambiguous and more error prone than that of the mere exchange of information between human and machine (Reilly, 1987). Interaction-like relationships between machines can be handled with relative ease, because machines are normally constructed with attention to prospective communication requirements. However, the similarly straightforward and technically established handling of emerging problems is unlikely when humans are communicating with each other.

Human-to-human interaction traditionally exploits standard communication modes which apply well-known verbal, written and gestural ways of transmitting and receiving explicit or implicit information. Here we investigate only those forms which utilise advanced computer technology -- especially the devices and tools of human-computer interaction.

1.1 *Key concepts*

It will be shown here that the achievements of computer technology (as well as of human-computer interaction theory and techniques) may increase greatly the efficiency and reliability of human-to-human communication -- especially if precision of transferred information is required. Therefore,

o   Human-computer interaction (i.e., combined human-to-computer and computer-to-human interaction) is examined to select features of highest potential benefit for the human-to-human interaction, and

o   Computer-supported means of human-to-human interaction are introduced, with the aim of applying computers as tools for the enhancement of communication between humans, and to achieve increased efficiency and reliability in the exact information exchange among humans as part of complex, cooperative man-machine systems.

Results of these two analyses may be summarised in the following corollaries.

o Human-computer interaction tools (human-computer interfaces) may be separated into human-to-computer and computer-to-human tools, each well distinguished by its basic tasks and properties. We shall call them human-to-computer interfaces (HCI) and computer-to-human interfaces (CHI).

o The separate human-to-computer and computer-to-human tools may be categorised with respect to human-centredness (i.e., with respect to their ability to handle human communication and to match human behaviour appropriately).

o Human-centred interaction tools are exploited easily in human-to-human communication/interaction.

o Computer-based interaction process human messages in an intentional manner.

o As a consequence, a computer-supported human-to-human interaction scheme can be introduced and applied widely, resulting in elevated efficiency and reliability for human-to-human information transfer. The suggested approach is called HCHI (human-computer-human interaction).

The key concept in HCHI is the intentional computer-based processing of human messages: intelligent machine support is provided to the human-to-human information transfer. This machine support covers not only the acquisition, storage, sorting, merging and retrieval of the transmitted information, but also the translation, formalisation, re-recording, analysis and re-synthesising of the human-to-human messages. Moreover, filtering, adjusting, correcting and storage of selected key facts from the messages also is involved. In this way, intelligent machines perform a transfer of related mental models by the suitable decoding/encoding of messages. Of course, HCHI in this context assumes that appropriate expertise and a knowledge base are built into the applied computers and interfaces (i.e., a form of AI-configured tools is postulated).

It will be shown that HCHI, by using human-centred interfaces as computer-based tools in information exchanges between humans, constitutes a new man-machine relationship. This new relationship enhances reliability, formal correctness and exactness (sometimes, even the adequacy and efficiency of the human-to-human interac-

tion). However, the price for these benefits in most cases is a somewhat rigid and mechanised style of interpersonal communication.

The suggested approach implies significant involvement by computerised tools in human communication, rather than the mere increase of convenience and efficiency of cooperation between the parties involved. Although the machine wouldn't usurp full control and regulation of human-to-human interaction, it would influence strongly the human communication process. The extent of this influence would depend both on the requirements and on practical implementation.

Several examples from the most feasible potential applications will be discussed. Some of these are simple utilisations of the suggested method (e.g., the exchange of mail between humans, the preparation of minutes of meetings and agreement memoranda, the control and correction of technical drawings, and the translation of man-made texts from one language into another). However, other utilisations discussed are truly sophisticated applications (e.g., information exchange among members of an engineering design team, communication between operators of a complex industrial system, and messaging between persons sharing tasks in traffic control). Still other potential applications of HCHI will only be mentioned in passing, without further detail (e.g., banking, medical practice, education, and the law).

1.2 *Chapter organisation*

In Section 2, the background for application of computer tools in enhancing human-to-human communication is discussed. Section 3 provides detail about human-centredness and HCHI concepts. Section 4 defines human-versus machine-centredness and Section 5 provides a brief commentary on the benefits and liabilities of HCHI, while in sections 6 and 7 further theoretical and practical aspects of HCHI are investigated. Section 8 deals with potential applications, while Section 9 addresses limited potential. Section 10 presents a set of open questions.

It should be noted that only the basic concepts of the HCHI method are discussed in this chapter. No actual, practical applications (or even working prototypes) are examined. Only some qualitative experiences (e.g., with CAD/CAM systems) attest to the usefulness of the HCHI approach. This chapter doesn't present quantitative analysis of experimental data. However, it is hoped that the discussion is sufficiently intriguing to motivate future work in the exactness and reliability of human-to-human interaction.

2. The characteristics of humans vs. machines

Human-computer interaction as a discipline has developed because of the many differences between humans and machines that are typical of man-machine systems (Callatay, 1986). Some of these differences are listed in Table 1.

Machine behaviour may be considered causal, whereas human behaviour is essentially non-causal. This means

Table 1. Pertinent differences between humans and machines

Property	Humans	Machines
Information exchange	Mostly verbal	Mostly formal
Information processing	Loose formalism	Firm formalism
Stress in information processing	Random/casual	Stable/regular
Communication	Coupled channels	Separate channels
Information processing determinism	Lacking	Present
Adaptability	Built-in	Limited
Capabilities	Changing	Fixed

Note: "Stress" signifies a very complex union of properties in sophisticated task-related behaviour and attitude, including disposition, inclination, focusing, concentration, care, apprehension, concern, pressure, and strain.

that machine input and output (I/O) relationships can be modelled well. However, no adequate models are available for the description of human I/O relationships. In other words, proper machine reactions to well-defined stimuli are exactly predictable (for all but the most complex cases), while prediction of human reactions -- even reactions to exactly defined changes of situation, circumstance, and motivation -- is extremely difficult.

These discrepancies between human and machine properties suggest two ideas. The first concerns the classification of human-to-computer and computer-to-human interfaces (in common: human-computer interfaces). The other is the potential for exploitation of machine characteristics in human-to-human interaction and communication. These concepts are introduced and investigated briefly in the following section.

3. The cases for machine (and human) involvement in communication

There are a large number of applications where machine-based systems require human intervention to achieve proper operation. The use of man-machine systems is made necessary by the fact that in most cases no fully automated operation can be achieved; computer-controlled subsystems are not able to cooperate correctly without the involvement of human operators. For example,

o Design automation without human participation could not be achieved even in the most straightforward technical problems (e.g., in electronics), be-

cause of the limitations of even the most complex physical models.

o Despite the high sophistication of on-board computers, without human intervention space vehicles couldn't manage appropriately the inevitable unexpected events during long space missions.

o Even by applying the most advanced automata and computer technology, nuclear power plants can't operate without human supervision, again because of the complexity of the technology.

The main reason machines fail in such situations is the inability to anticipate all possible events in the models upon which their operating systems are based, in any high complexity circumstance.

Requirements for human-to-human as well as human-computer interaction also depend on the situation and circumstances under consideration. In general, the demands typical of human and/or machine activity stem from qualitative and quantitative task complexity, reaction speed requirements, spatial properties of events, the well- or ill-conditioned character of required actions, and the complexity and coverage of models implemented in machine support. From this, one can conclude that

o Human judgment is essential if qualitative complexity is not addressed adequately by computerised models, or if the machine is ill-conditioned for possible events and required actions.

o Machine involvement is necessary if rapid decisions are needed and/or the spatial distribution of events doesn't allow human perception of all related parameters. (It also is necessary if quantitative complexity restricts or prohibits purely human evaluation.)

o In all other cases, either humans or machines alone are able to perform the required job acceptably, provided that no extra parameters and no additional event types become involved in the decisions and/or actions undertaken.

However, because of the theoretically unlimited number of (closely or loosely) related parameters and the finite probability of unforeseen events, virtually any practical applications for which purely machine operation might be assumed still should involve human supervision or participation.

Despite the commonly held conviction that human-machine interaction is a must in virtually all machine-implemented systems -- and that this kind of interaction poses many theoretical and practical problems -- it is rarely recognised that similar problems arise in cooperation between humans. However, an important understanding has emerged recently: Acknowledgment that exactness and reliability in the collaboration of humans as system components may be enhanced considerably enhanced by introducing computers into the human-to-human interaction processes (much as the introduction of humans into machine-to-machine interaction-based systems is helpful).

Consequently, the basic precept of this chapter is the introduction of the computer as an intermediary component in the human-to-human transfer of information, both in cases of purely human-to-human interaction and of man-machine systems including several cooperating humans.

This involvement of computers in human-to-human communication procedures (i.e., the use of "HCHI" rather than traditional HHI and HCI/CHI schema) requires a special approach to interfaces -- an approach which at first sight may seem to be strange. (Why complicate the natural and traditional means of human communication?) However, the properties of human-to-human information exchange and the requirements posed in many cases for this exchange make necessary a new way of aiding humans in some interactions and cooperation.

Consider the following three arguments why the introduction of such computer-based communication aids is required.

o First, the number of operational systems in which inappropriate decisions and actions may result in serious failures or even disasters (e.g., in industry, traffic, banking, and medical systems) is increasing rapidly. Adequate and precise information exchange between humans is a must in such systems.

o Second, the complexity of most operational systems also is increasing rapidly, requiring machine support in human-to-human information transfer (e.g., in data acquisition, storage, filtering, selection, and retrieval).

o Third, human attitudes, behaviour and cultural backgrounds are evolving continuously. Individuals become increasingly unique, with disparate knowledge, experiences, motivation and habits. Thus, a shared understanding of what human messages mean and imply requires the more formal support provided by computerised tools.

4. Human-centred vs. machine-centred human-computer interfaces

As we have seen, human-computer interfaces play an important role in HCHI. Human nature (human cognition and emotional behaviour) are important aspects in the construction of such interfaces.

The classification of HCHI interfaces suggested below is based on the relationship of the interface characteristics to aspects presented in Table 1 (including how interfaces behave and what properties they have with respect to human characteristics).

Interfaces may be either human-centred (capable of dealing with human nature and behaviour) or machine-centred (built by applying formal, rigid interaction schema in order to facilitate system construction).

Human-centred interfaces attempt to bridge the gap between human and machine properties, while machine-centred interfaces presume machine-like human properties (therefore cannot bridge a wide human-machine gap).

Of course, constructing machine-centred interfaces is much easier than constructing human-centred interfaces, but machine-centred interfaces require much more adaptation by humans (familiarity with computer usage is assumed).

Machine-centred interfaces may be constructed either intentionally (i.e., based consciously on a cost-related selection of a machine-centred rather than human-centred solution), or because of the lack of resources required for the more demanding task of constructing a human-centred interface.

The HCHI principle described in Section 3 presumes the use of human-centred interfaces. Application of this principle and of human-centredness is key to exploiting the potential of computers in making human-to-human information exchange efficient and reliable without assuming too much human familiarity with computers.

5. HCHI vs. competing paradigms

The intent behind introduction of the HCHI approach (and of human-centred interfaces) is to establish a new man-machine relationship. Via this relationship, human-to-human communication would become more reliable, more formal and more exact, although more rigid and more mechanised.

The need to apply HCHI depends on how important exactness is in information traffic between humans. Such exactness seems to be most important in technical information exchange (situations in which facts and data may play a critical role in adequate communication).

The idea of introducing computers into human-to-human communication is not entirely new. It has been attempted in several practical applications, especially when humans are distant from each other in time and/or space. However, in most cases the unaltered recording or transparent transmission of human messages is the only aim; no intentional filtering is involved. The key differences between such earlier attempts and HCHI are that HCHI is targeted at

o allowing a more general approach to all cases of

human communication that require exactness, and

o allowing intentional computer-based intelligent processing of the human messages.

Despite its newness, the concept of HCHI may seem at the first sight to be somewhat familiar to those who are involved in one area of man-machine theory and practice: computer-supported cooperative work (CSCW). This rapidly evolving discipline also seeks to aid individuals by using computers in human cooperation (Bowers, 1991; Galegher, 1990).

However, CSCW encompasses only one of the many practical applications of HCHI. It concentrates on human collaboration with the aim of achieving a well defined goal related to a specific activity, or of solving a well defined task.

HCHI may be useful in a much wider spectrum of human-to-human communication and interaction, especially in relation to operation of complex man-machine systems. It differs from CSCW in its objective (aiding interpretation of human-to-human communication/interaction versus merely supporting cooperative work). Therefore, HCHI must entail the significant involvement of computerised tools (e.g., intelligent interfaces and an AI-configured machine), for many essential information processing tasks. CSCW, on the other hand, provides instrumentation merely for increasing the convenience and efficiency of communication and cooperation among the parties involved.

Table 2 contrasts HCHI to traditional HHI (human-to-human interaction), HCI/CHI (combined human-to-computer and computer-to-human interaction) and CSCW.

Table 2. Characteristics of competing interface paradigms

Characteristic	HHI	HCI/CHI	CSCW	HCHI
Efficiency	high	low	medium	medium
Reliability	low	medium	medium	high
Cost	low	high	high	medium
Limitations	many	average	average	few
Applications	wide	limited	bounded	wide
Future horizon	wide	medium	medium	wide
Open questions	few	many	average	many

Analysis of Table 2 indicates that HCHI may be inferior to HHI in terms of efficiency, cost and the extent of open questions, and to CSCW in terms of open questions. However, considering typical applications and normal circumstances, HCHI appears to be superior to the other interface paradigms in terms of other characteristics. The many open questions related to HCHI should be taken as a warning about the lack of immediate feasibility of applying HCHI in candidate applications.

6. Properties and applications of the HCHI approach

The introduction of computers into human-to-human information transfer as intermediary components is affected by two sets of factors: (a) the distinctive properties of human and machine participants in man-computer interaction, and (b) the situations that are characteristic of information exchange if humans are interacting with humans.

The computer intermediary is a crucial tool of the HCHI approach. The enhancement achievable by means of this computer support is based on the capability of the introduced machine to transmit not only the formulated messages, but also the mental models of individuals involved in the human-to-human communication. This transfer of mental models is useful in decoding/encoding the messages correctly within context. Computer processing can filter, adjust, and correct messages as well as store key facts deduced from them. Of course, such interpretative processing assumes appropriate expertise and a related knowledge base as part of applied interfaces. In other words, HCHI presumes an AI configuration (Barr, 1986 & 1989; Partridge, 1990).

Potential applications (discussed in detail in sections 7 and 9) include

o Industrial systems, in which humans should perform tasks with an exactness matching that of the technological processes themselves.

o Medical practice, where patient survival sometimes depends on the precise and clear exchange of information among cooperating doctors and assistants.

o Business and financial administration, where the accurate and trustworthy transfer of high fidelity information between humans is of key importance.

In fact, it is hard to find any field of human activity or functions of man-machine systems in which there is no long-range feasibility of exploiting benefits provided by HCHI. In the short term, however, the picture is somewhat less optimistic.

First, HCHI is not a cheap technique. Second, there are many open theoretical and technical questions regarding true HCHI solutions. And third, the implementation and dissemination of such an approach requires a long time. (Practical realisations will disperse slowly, appearing initially only in crucial applications.)

The main differences between human- and machine-centred interface realisations are found in how information is forwarded from the source (human or computer) to the target (computer or human).

In the case of a human-to-computer interface, the system may transform human output (e.g., written or spoken messages) into a form acceptable as machine input. Alternatively, the interface may use fixed form (i.e., machine-centred) information transfer, which requires adaptation by the human to rules dictated by the computer behind the interface. In free form (i.e., human-centred) information transfer, the interface should interpret messages received from the human agent, regardless of form.

In the case of a computer-to-human interface, the system may transform machine output (e.g., data files) into a form acceptable as human input (i.e., human-perceivable signals and messages). Output towards the human would be of fixed form. The degree of human-centredness of the interface would depend on whether the interface was ready to adapt to human needs. Such adaptation may allow freedom for the human, by making his or her interpretation and understanding of output as natural as possible.

In order to be truly human-centred, an interface must have

o Nearly free-form command input (e.g., example, there is no assumption of menu-driven or direct manipulation operation).

o Nearly free-form natural language input (e.g., no reliance on a limited, keyword vocabulary).

o Nearly free-form graphical manipulation (i.e., no fixed form techniques for editing graphical constructs and drawings are required).

o Nearly free-form gestural input (i.e., for multimedia systems, no limited gesture set is presumed).

The introduction of computers into human-to-human communication with the aim of achieving the necessary degree of interpretation and filtering requires the most flexible and adaptive human-centred interfaces.

Although adaptivity and flexibility doubtless are crucial elements in human-centred interfaces, they are not the only properties of a truly human-centred interface. Such interfaces must be able to

o Recognise most forms of human communication (e.g., sound or movement).

o Comprehend a wide variety of background cultures (e.g., via use of a semantic analyser) and allow for several education levels.

o Manage error checking and control (plus acknowledgement) of many kinds of transformed/processed messages.

o Take over some human actions in case of the human's inability to continue communication and interaction.

Under what circumstances may we call machine involvement "significant" in the sense of mediating communication (versus being only a convenience of information transfer)? Building upon the previous discussion, it can be stated that the involvement of computer-based tools should be considered significant if

o Machine support to the human-to-human information transfer includes acquisition, storage, sorting, merging and retrieval of transmitted information;

o Translation, formalisation, re-recording, analysis and re-synthesising of the human-to-human messages is included in the machine functions;

o Computer processing involves filtering, adjusting and correcting (as well as storage) of selected key facts from the messages;

o The transfer of mental models is performed with high fidelity via suitable decoding/encoding of messages, and

o Appropriate expertise (i.e., some form of artificial intelligence) and a related knowledge-base are built into the applied computers/interfaces.

Systems that satisfy these criteria should be considered true HCHI solutions.

7. HCHI in practice: how to apply the suggested approach

On the basis of the HCHI principle, a new man-machine relationship may be established, allowing more reliable, more formal and more exact exchanges of information.

The realisation of HCHI would feature HCI and CHI interfaces acting as intermediaries in human-to-human communication. These interfaces would act as catalysts, and mediate or negotiate between humans. Such involvement is possible for any manned system in which human-to-human interaction is a critical element in operation of the system.

In traditional HCI practice, discrepancies between human and machine are considered inconvenient, and problems stemming from these discrepancies are to be avoided or eliminated, if possible. The HCHI approach addresses such discrepancies directly. The properties which are lacking (causality, formalism, homogeneity, channel separation and determinism) are provided by the mediating machine negotiator. This makes it possible for human messages to be coordinated, adjusted and integrated by the more rigid machine cooperator. The computerised HCHI tool would enhance human-to-human communication in cooperation with humans users by improving the quality of message transfer and by increasing the reliability, precision and situated context of message interpretation for recipients.

A critical feature of HCHI would be its ability to introduce formalised protocols into communication among humans. Such protocols may be adjusted to user needs and preferences. Despite being adjustable, however, such protocols would retain exactness. In most cases, HCHI systems should allow (even motivate or force) originating humans to validate interpretations before messages are forwarded. Such validation is especially important in terms of the key facts extracted from messages.

8. Applications: from bilateral conversation to complex systems

A wide spectrum of man-machine systems rely heavily on human-to-human interaction and on the quality and outcome of human-to-human communication. Instances include information exchange among members of an engineering design team, communication between operators of a complex industrial system, and message transactions between individuals sharing tasks in traffic control. In addition to such systems, future HCHI may benefit fields as diverse as banking, medical practice, education and law. Although it may be difficult to implement HCHI in such fields, all include activities for which the exactness and reliability of human-to-human information transfer are of key importance.

Despite implementation difficulties in such fields, there are some very simple everyday applications amenable to HCHI. These include

o Interpersonal correspondence (The correctness of grammar and style could be evaluated and corrected by the computer, and facts (dates and times, places) verified.

o Minutes of meetings and agreement memoranda (The correctness, precision and completeness of information could be checked. The extent of verification should depend on how much intelligence was provided by the knowledge base and AI inference engine.)

o Man-made texts from non-technical fields (These could be translated from one language to another, ensuring the at times important equivalence of source and target texts. However, truly effective machine-supported translation would need to mirror the full intent and cultural context of those communicating -- a capability that probably won't be achieved in the near future.)

There also are a number of crucial industrial applications that could be improved by HCHI, from simple graphical information exchange to the most complex design and planning activities (Begg, 1984; Cushman, 1991).

o Technical drawings (especially sketches) for communication between engineering and technical staff in industrial organisations. (Filtering and correcting graphical information media would be important to achieving error-free technical information exchange.)

o Integrated functional, electrical and physical designs of electronic systems and circuits -- for example, drawings, master artworks, and numerical control files for production/testing. (This process often suffers as a result of uncontrolled interactions among functional, electrical and packaging designers. HCHI could add desperately needed formalism to the communication process.)

o Engineering (product) design and process (technology) planning (technological planning) in manufacturing organisations. (Contradictions between design concepts/targets and associated manufacturing processes sometimes result in a failure to meet original specifications. HCHI could help avoid misunderstandings and misinterpretations.)

9. HCHI's limitations

Despite its advantages and potential for widespread application, care should be taken in terms of where and when HCHI is used. Its most important limitations, weaknesses and shortcomings should be kept in mind.

o HCHI probably will be an expensive technique, especially in the early stages of it's application. (Human-centred interfaces are expensive, in general.)

o Many open theoretical and technical questions still must be answered before true HCHI solutions can be achieved.

o The wide dissemination of HCHI principles can be anticipated only in the long range. Practical applications will emerge slowly and sporadically, especially during the start-up period.

o At the beginning, HCHI solutions probably will appear only in critical applications. The first proofs of concept probably will be the most demanding man-machine systems (those that require exact and precise human-to-human information exchange).

o The first HCHI implementations predictably will suffer from users' feelings of being inconvenienced, an effect introduced by the approach itself. Until truly efficient solutions appear, users may feel that this new way of communicating is irritating and disturbing, compared to traditional (informal) human-to-human interaction. The effect is similar to that observed in even the simplest cases of introducing computer techniques to traditional organisations and operations (Card, 1986; Salvendy, 1987).

10. The open questions

In all potential application areas, misunderstandings, disregarded messages and a lack of information frequently cause virtually unavoidable problems -- problems which might be bypassed through the use of HCHI. However, there remain a number of open questions regarding computer-aided human-to-human interaction.

o Is it feasible today to develop the amount of intelligence, expertise and knowledge necessary to realise true HCHI solutions?

o Is HCHI truly different from HCI/CHI and CSCW, or is HCHI merely a tangential approach benefiting from the successes of other paradigms?

o Are humans ready to communicate/interact with each other by using HCHI-type support, or will resistance with respect to such a novel "tool" prohibit HCHI's introduction in the near term?

o What truly straightforward applications of the HCHI principle are possible in the near future (if any)?

o Is it possible to model human characteristics, habits, behaviour and cognition in such a way that they can be represented in and manipulated by likely AI configurations supporting the computer/interface?

o Is the potential cost/benefit ratio sufficient to permit/validate the application of HCHI in practical applications -- at least in critical industrial man-machine systems characterised by a high risk of potential disaster?

Answering these questions -- by building a broader theoretical foundation and conducting practical experiments -- may help to advance the chances for successful and wide-ranging future applications of the HCHI approach.

Acknowledgments

This paper is based on a talk presented by the author at the People and Computers VIII conference (HCI'93) in Loughborough, UK, during September 1993. Thanks are due to all who provided a preliminary critique and who made comments regarding the paper, especially to Donald L. Day for his support and assistance. The author also would like to express his thanks to the Hungarian National Research Fund (OTKA) for supporting the related research.

References

BARR, A., COHEN, P.R., AND FEIGENBAUM, E.A. 1986 & 1989, *Handbook of Artificial Intelligence*, Vols. 1 & 4. (Addison-Wesley, Reading, Mass).

BAYLEY, R.W. 1982, *Human Performance Engineering: A Guide for System Designers*. (Prentice Hall, Englewood Cliffs, N.J.).

BEGG, V. 1984, *Making Computer Aided Design Tools More Usable: A Study of A Complex Task Shared By People and Machines*. (Kogan Page, London).

BOWERS, J.M. & BENFORD, S.D. (eds) 1991, *Studies in Computer Supported Cooperative Work: Theory, Practice and Design*. (North-Holland, Amsterdam).

CALLATAY, A.M. 1986, *Natural and Artificial Intelligence*. (Elsevier, Amsterdam).

CARD, S.K., MORAN, I.P., & NEWELL, A. 1986, *The Psychology of Human-Computer Interaction*. (Lawrence Erlbaum, Hillsdale, N.J.).

CUSHMAN, W.H. & ROSENBERG, D.J. 1991, *Human Factors in Product Design*. (Elsevier, Amsterdam).

GALEGHER, J., KRAUT, R., & EGIDO, C. (eds) 1990, *Intellectual Teamwork: Social and Technological Foundations of Cooperative Work*. Lawrence Erlbaum, Hillsdale, N.J.).

HELANDER, M. (ed) 1988, *Handbook of Human-Computer Interaction*. (North-Holland, Amsterdam).

PARTRIDGE, D. & WILKS, Y. (eds) 1990, *The Foundation of Artificial Intelligence*. (Cambridge University Press, Cambridge, Mass.).

RASMUSSEN, J. & ANDERSEN, H.B. 1991, *Human-Computer Interaction*. (Lawrence Erlbaum, Hillsdale, N.J.).

REILLY, R.G. (ed) 1987, *Communication Failure in Dialogue and Discourse*. (Elsevier, Amsterdam).

SALVENDY, G. (ed) 1987, *Social, Ergonomic and Stress Aspects of Work with Computers*. (Elsevier, Amsterdam).

VICKERS, D. & SMITH, P.L. (eds) 1989, *Human Information Processing: Measures, Mechanisms and Models*. (Elsevier, Amsterdam).

Part 2: Knowledge Representation

4

Mapping the mapper

JOHN WOOD AND PAUL TAYLOR

Goldsmiths College, University of London, Lewisham Way, New Cross, London SE14 6NW, UK
j.wood@gold.ac.uk

(Appendix by ALESSIO QUARZO-CERINA)

Abstract. This chapter describes aspects of the IDEAbase project, a novel hypertext environment intended to assist researchers and students of art and design. For this group, the significant mode of knowledge is tacit rather than theoretical, deriving more from the 'task-centred' or applied mindset of the medieval craft guilds tradition than from the 'epistemology-centred' or scholastic mindset of the monastic disciplines. Nonetheless, studio-based artists and designers increasingly need to inform their responsible practices with scholastic knowledge, normally available in the form of serial text.

1. Introduction

For artists and designers, the clash between task-centred and epistemology-centred approaches to knowledge representation is evident in many ways, including library retrieval problems and the absence of agreed source mapping methods. This chapter discusses one solution, a hypertext environment (IDEAbase) in which information is mapped as a multi-dimensional network before being encoded into a document.

The mathematical concept of mapping is the key to the IDEAbase project, which in this example attempts to map the ideas and designs of Buckminster Fuller -- who himself developed maps (actual geographical maps and intellectual maps of fields of study relevant to design). In conjunction with a mapping of Fuller's totalistic conception of design thinking, in this example the notion of mapping itself underpins an application of Peirce's (1960) notion of abduction -- here construed as a mechanism for conceptual development and problem-solving.

The facilities afforded by hypertext enable the IDEAbase user mapping the range of concerns presented by Fuller to relate disparate ideas abductively in such a way that s/he becomes aware of the issue of mapping itself. The user thereby is increasingly self-aware of the mappings developed during interaction with this hypertext environment.

IDEAbase helps the user generally to develop a mental map of the inter-relationships among the various fields and ideas relevant to specific issues of concern. Beyond this, however, lie questions of mapping and modelling specific to the subject matter of the hypertext being studied. Fuller's geometrical theories can be investigated conveniently in this form, can be tested, and can be applied to other aspects of his work (as well as to other design questions).

2. Background

2.1 *The nature of studio practice*

It is important to highlight the salient differences between 'creative practices' of the studio and those of other professions. Schön (1985) points to the historical schism between scholastic research-based methods and those evolved by practice-oriented professionals such as doctors, architects and designers. These differences can be traced to their roots in the mediaeval monastic and craft guild institutions respectively, resulting in disparate epistemologies.

The significant modes of knowledge used by artists and designers in their creative practice include 'tacit knowledge', received wisdom, and skills of judgement acquired through practical experience in the studio. By contrast, the traditional scholastic essay is linear and sequential, employing such devices such as syllogistic logic.

Historically speaking, "silent" reading is a comparatively recent skill; it is likely that the form of the scholastic essay evolved from the rhetoric of public speaking.

Therefore, it is inclined to elevate the status of the author by permitting the creation of a fresh thesis from the bones of extant writings. For this reason, it is de rigour for academic authors to cite precedent as a potential claim to authority, traditionally in the form of gods, heroes, famous men, distinguished authors and (more recently) in bibliographic data. This may explain the emphasis upon accurate sourcing and serial development strategies in academic writing. Likewise, 'scholastic rigour' is a key attribute of such writing, attained only through impeccable clarity and explicitness of argumentation.

This notion of "rigour" can be inappropriate for many art and design practices. Their genres and methods emphasise qualities that may be difficult to analyse in words. Many emphasise visual attributes and celebrate novelty. For artists and designers, social acceptance more often derives from a range of attributes judged by outcome rather than by methodology. Therefore, the capabilities of the artist/designer are a fusion of tacit and intellectual abilities (such as skills of judgement, problem-solving, organisation and manipulation of materials). Design sometimes is described as a form of rhetoric. In this sense, design solutions often appear to flaunt their own 'problem solving' capacity in a conspicuous or celebratory way.

Nevertheless, modern artists and designers increasingly need to inform responsible practice with theoretical support, in the form of scholastic knowledge. The continuing changes to studio practice mean that a modern counterpart of the "master craftsman" may no longer be the recipient of the essential wealth of oral knowledge. Rapidly changing technologies have brought hitherto unforeseen problems (and possibilities). Environmental and ethical problems, in particular, have made theory an increasingly vital component of design. Obviously, this type of knowledge is available only in critical, analytical and logical modes, usually presented in long strings of textual argumentation. It is tempting to suggest that a more relevant form of knowledge would be polysemic rather than monosemic, and intuitive rather than rule-based.

For all of these reasons, it is not unusual to find that the immediate concerns of an artist's studio project have an apparently tenuous connection with parallel interests in theory.

This is hardly surprising, as a major difficulty confronting artists and designers is that ideas and information that may be relevant to specific projects often are dispersed across a wide range of disciplines. As a result, many practitioners find themselves overwhelmed by time-consuming problems of library retrieval -- in particular, the absence of agreed source mapping methods. Artists and designers often are uncertain which information domain will be relevant in clarifying particular problems or in reaching fresh solutions.

It has been shown that in the early phases of creative design, it actually may be unhelpful to predict the sequence of decisions toward solutions. In this sense, there may be no general correspondence between a given studio problem and a seemingly relevant tract of text from scholastic sources.

Arguably, these factors could account in part for the popularity of post-structuralist and de-constructionist texts in the art and design community; they appear to offer a semantically richer, more ambiguous, and therefore creatively more stimulating domain than that of (classical) "scientific" or linear historical argument.

The concepts of 'mapping' and 'modelling' offer important alternatives to conventions of serial text representation, since they emulate more closely the mechanisms by which deeds can be explored (either in advance, retrospectively, or at a distance), by means of symbolic or functional representation. The term "mental models" has been used in AI research to denote propositional models formed, manipulated or tested outside of the mind of the user. For example, Johnson-Laird (1985) has claimed that "Mental models provide a basis for representing premises, and their manipulation makes it possible to reason without logic."

2.2 *Hypertext in the design studio*

Vannevar Bush, a scientific adviser to President Roosevelt, is credited with the original inspiration for hypertext. In 1945, aware of the explosive growth of new technologies, of available information, and in general of the "summation of human experience", Bush called for development of a new type of "mechanised private file and library". He had become impressed by the new psychological principle of "associationism" and wanted a system that could work the way the human mind does. He envisaged a mechanical device with which users could make their own associative leaps, creating mnemonic codes and "connecting" data items together into information "trails". Later pioneers who developed working systems claimed that these methods actually could enlarge the scope of human thought (Engelbart, 1963) and empower human memory (Nelson, 1980).

Unfortunately, some studies have suggested that in a general learning context hypertext may be no more effective than paper-based documents. However, the imperatives of the studio can differ significantly from those of a conventional classroom; it is doubtful whether readership by 'action-oriented' artists and designers is comparable to the readership of more 'theory-oriented' scholars. One of the celebrated attributes of hypertext is its "non-linearity". The user can choose to read in many alternative directions. S/he therefore may read in a way that is more chaotic, yet more immediately result-oriented.

Barrett (1989) describes hypertext as "an a-cyclic, asynchronous sharing of language around central topics of concern". Whilst this notion may seem dubious to some academically trained scholars, it is curiously inviting to artists or designers who are eager for ambiguity (a more interrogative and polysemic form of stimulation). For this reason, we are persuaded that hypertext can serve effectively to inform art and design studio practice -- even if it has failed so far to find unqualified approval in a more orthodox learning context. Carlson (1990) and others have drawn attention to the radical rhetorical nature of hypertext, reminding us that all revolutions are likely to have both positive and negative effects on society. Nevertheless, we are hopeful that once an appropriate IDEAbase system is tailored to the needs of a specific community of artists or designers, a corpus of locally edited ideas will accrue that will encourage sound creative collaboration. We plan to establish this potential across (and beyond) the campus electronic network.

3. IDEAbase

IDEAbase was initiated in 1990 as an ongoing programme of research and software development using ideas inspired by hypertext. The first four letters of "IDEAbase" are an acronym for the "Interactive Database of Enabling Arguments". The project's principal aim is to help designers and artists author and exchange documentary material that may enhance the culture of ideas and creative practice in an academic community. The design of the system is tailored to the distinctive needs of this group, whose professional vernacular is more ad hoc, context-dependent and flexible in its taxonomy than many others. To meet these needs, an inexpensive Hypertext authoring system was developed to enable authors to convert text-based documents into a hypertext format within which semantic correspondences would be established automatically and dynamically (within and between documents). The system enables other authors and readers to access related ideas from within IDEAbase documents.

Unlike most hypertext systems there is no provision for creating discrete hypertext 'links' in IDEAbase documents. This was found to be too distracting and laborious. Instead, authors do most writing using favourite "word processing" applications. They simply add headings and keywords and mark "associated terms" with SGML (Standard Generalised Mark-Up Language) codes. The system then converts the marked-up text into an interactive "IDEAbase" structure, which locates relevant associations dynamically.

IDEAbase offers no methodological guidelines for the form that documents should take or for the types of associations that may be made between ideas and terms. Nevertheless, the mechanisms of interaction within and between documents is effective irrespective of whether authored associations are made spontaneously or on a systematic basis. The simplicity and flexibility of IDEAbase thus fosters and sustains a heterogeneous community of authors and readers.

Authors can make modifications either by returning to the original WP document or by choosing to work from within the IDEAbase environment, using built-in editing tools. A key feature of IDEAbase is its ability to make both "explicit sense" and "implicit sense" concordances, either within one document or between documents. As a result, it provides an excellent platform for distance learning, staff training, collaborative authorship, and interdisciplinary research and publication.

4. Creation of the Fuller Network

One of the projects developed as a prototype for IDEAbase was the "Fuller Network". The first phase of the Fuller Network was undertaken by Paul Taylor in 1991. It began with the compilation of various ideas, principles, designs and domains of interest drawn from the work of the distinguished designer Richard Buckminster Fuller. The network was founded chiefly by the augmentation, concatenation and creation of indexes to Fuller's writings. The 480 items thus compiled were arranged graphically and were interconnected (on paper) by lines of relation such as equivalence, kinship, subsumption, etc. This process yielded a non-sequential, multi-dimensional network of interconnected items or nodes, each of which then was developed into a textual module in a hypertext document.

In the next phase, this graphic "map" was written into software form using Prolog, "front-ended" with Hyper-Card. By framing questions about the relationships among nodes (e.g., "What is the connection between 'Tensegrity Structures' and 'Total Thinking'?"), the program presented a series of annotated "pathways" representing every concept node encountered along the "route" to a particular node.

5. Computer aided design thinking

The Fuller Network helps design thinking in the following ways:

1. It presents a detailed case study of the comprehensive designer.

2. It shows how certain theoretical matters may be related to practical design (e.g., how geometrical ideas are applied to architecture and cartography).

3. It provides check lists of factors relevant to design.

4. It discusses problem-solving and heuristics.

5. It enables the abductive formation of new conceptions of disparate design issues.

6. It enables rhythmically modulated interaction be-

tween the user and the contents of the network.

6. Mapping

This application of mapping follows the simple approach advocated by March and Steadman (1971): "A given set of data only acquires significance when we map it onto a pattern of some kind". The data may be (as Sanford, 1985, says) "sensory information, the perception of events, fragments of discourse, and so on". They are mapped onto what he calls "appropriate information in memory". In Sanford's terms, the mapping is made onto

> a whole conglomerate of information which is useful and readily and rapidly accessed. By assuming that information is organised in appropriate bundles, with the relationships between the bundles made readily accessible, the mapping process seems to be much easier to understand. The bundles are variously known as scripts, frames and schemata.

March and Steadman argue that

> a new pattern will be recognised only by an observer who has available, or who develops, an appropriate range of mental sets, abstract or otherwise, upon which to map the data.

They give the example of the mapping of otherwise troublesome observations onto a non-Euclidean geometrical framework, leading to the famous explanation known as Relativity Theory. They also offer a converse case: the report given by Captain Cook of the Australian aborigines' inability to "see" his ship approach their shore (due to their lack of an appropriate receiving matrix).

7. Mapping the mapper

Richard Buckminster Fuller was a mapper in two broad senses. He made an original contribution to cartography by developing a new projection, with which he produced a minimally distorting map of the world. Fuller used this "Dymaxion Map" to present ideas and information about global energy supplies and traffic patterns. Beyond this, however, he was concerned about many issues, physical, social and conceptual, which impinge on design. In this sense, he was mapping factors onto an intellectual matrix that purported to be a totalistic conception of design.

The reflexive self-awareness entailed in such an approach to design can be appreciated by exploration of the network. This appreciation is fostered partly by gradual acquaintance with Fuller's work, and partly by the fact that what takes place as a result of interaction with the network is development of new mappings of information onto the user's mental schemata. In addition, the issues of

mapping and modelling are discussed explicitly in the text itself.

8. Abduction

The notion of *mapping* can be related to the higher-order notion of abduction, which is of crucial importance to construing the modus operandi of the IDEAbase network.

Abduction is a kind of inference that is neither deduction nor induction. It is a process whereby a surprising fact is made explicable by the application of a suitable proposition. Abduction is attributed to C.S. Peirce: "A surprising fact, C, is observed. But if a proposition, A, were true, C would be a matter of course. Hence, there is a reason to suspect that A is true."

Rowe (1987) quotes Peirce and adds that

> abduction includes the case where A and C are distinct from one another and only become related through the existence of some appropriated scheme, or 'view of the world', that has meaning for both A and C.

Abduction is, in Rowe's terms,

> an appropriation from outside the problem space, used for its promise of providing a higher level of organisation. For instance, a designer at the outset of tackling a problem in housing may decide to make use of a particular type of configuration. Furthermore, that type becomes the model through which the problem is understood and construed.

Rowe goes on to relate abduction to heuristics. The abductive

> mode of inquiry is very common in design. We often employ heuristics that allow us to import autonomous constraints into our problem spaces in order to facilitate further activity. In fact, in the case of ill-defined and wicked problems abduction is the rule rather than the exception.

9. Conclusion

The relating of information among disparate domains is facilitated by the IDEAbase network. This process is facilitated using the mapping paradigm, which in turn is the basis for abduction. Thus, the user is helped towards solving design problems by means of the new mappings invoked by the IDEAbase network.

References

BARRETT, E., 1989, *The Society of Text* (MIT Press, Cambridge, MA), xiii.

BROWN, J.S. 1982, "Notes Concerning Desired Functionality, Issues and Philosophy for an Authoring Land", CIS Working Paper (Xerox Park, Palo Alto, CA).

BRUFFEE, K.A. (1988), Liberal education and the social justification in belief, *Liberal Education* **68**, 95-114.

BUCCIARELLI, 1991 (July), An ethnographic perspective on engineering design, *Design Studies* **9** (3), 159-168.

BUSH, V., 1945, As we may think, *Atlantic Monthly* **7**.

CARLSON, P.A. 1990, The rhetoric of hypertext, *Hypermedia* **2**, 115.

DOLAND, V.M. 1989 (Spring), Hypermedia as an interpretative act, *Hypermedia*, 6-19.

DREYFUS, H.L. & DREYFUS, S.E., 1986, "Mind over Machine; The Power of Human Intuition in the era of the computer" (Basil Backwell, UK).

ENGELBART, D., 1963, A conceptual framework for the augmentation of man's intellect, in *Vistas in Information Handling* (Spartan Books, London).

FRISSE, M. 1988, From text to hypertext, *Byte* **13** (10), 247-253.

FULLER, B. 1976, *Synergetics* (MacMillan, London).

JOHNSON-LAIRD, P.N., 1985, Mental models, 98, in Aitkenhead, A.M., & Slack, J.M, *Issues in Cognitive Modelling* (Lawrence Erlbaum, Sussex, UK).

LAWSON, B., AND ROBERTS, S.; Modes and features: the organisation of data in CAD supporting the early phases of design, *Design Studies Journal* **12** (2), 102-108.

MARCH, L. & STEADMAN, P. 1971, "The Geometry of Environment" (London), 29.

McKNIGHT, C., DILLON, A., & RICHARDSON, J. 1989 (June), A comparison of linear and hypertext formats in information retrieval, in *Hypertext II Conference Proceedings* (University of York, UK).

NELSON, T.H., 1980 (October), Replacing the printed word: a complete literary system. *IFIP Proceedings*, 1013-1023

PEIRCE, C.S. 1960, *Collected Papers of Charles Peirce* (C. Hartshorne & P. Weiss, eds) (Harvard University Press, Cambridge, MA), 374, f.

POLANYI, M. (1969), Tacit knowing, in *Knowing and Being*, (Routledge & Kegan Paul, London).

ROWE, P.G. 1987, *Design Thinking* (MIT Press, Cambridge, MA),102.

RYLE, G., 1949, On knowing how and knowing that", in *The Concept of Mind* (Hutcheson, London).

SANFORD, A.J.: 1985, *Cognition And Cognitive Psychology* (London), 205.

SCHÖN, D., *The Design Studio* (RIBA Publications Ltd., London).

WARNOCK , M. 1976, *Imagination* (Faber & Faber, London & Boston), 30.

WOOD, J. & CLARKE, J. 1993 (July), "A Convivial Authoring Environment for Researchers in Art & Design", conference paper, Prolog in Education Group '93, Heriot Watt University, Edinburgh.

WOOD, J. 1990, "The IDEAbase Project at Goldsmiths' College: Browsing for One's Own Ideas", in Autumn Collection, Kings College Computing Centre Publication, 3.

WOOD, J. 1990 (July), The socially responsible designer, *Design International Journal*, 5.

Appendix

A preliminary evaluation of IDEAbase

ALESSIO QUARZO-CERINA

Goldsmiths College, University of London

1. Introduction

This appendix summarises a survey conducted by Alessio Quarzo-Cerina, an independent qualitative researcher specialising in the advertising and product development industry. It describes an attempt to provide user feedback about the IDEAbase project, through qualitative research. The principal objective of this research was to ascertain the relevance and appeal of a non-linear, intuitive software environment such as IDEAbase in the context of designers' culture and practices, especially in relation to knowledge.

While the concepts that frame the arguments in this survey were taken directly from the article "Mapping the mapper", our key concern was to understand whether such concepts bear any resemblance to the way designers go about and conceive of their work, on their terms.

2. Methodology

Four in-depth interviews of approximately one hour each were conducted with designers, following a broad and holistic design course at Goldsmiths' College, University of London. The sample was chosen deliberately. Interviews were split between male and female respondents; all were required to be at least computer literate.

The interviews took the form of a collaborative process between moderator and respondent, during which the various relevant issues were covered and concepts were tested.

3. Key findings

1. As designers, respondents distinguish themselves from artists in that they did not conceive of the objects they created merely as signifiers in a social space. They saw them as functioning as effective and relevant solutions to identifiable problems.

2. Respondents spoke of design as a mix of the subjective and objective, of knowledge and gut feel, of art and craft. Their work thus is characterised by an eclecticism and an holistic approach to research, method and creative judgement.

4. Respondents' creative methods

4.1 *Eclectic and holistic approaches*

Respondents testified to the eclectic and holistic method they use in 'researching' their work. For example, they admitted to "working backwards as well as forwards", and to jumping into a problem space at any point, depending on whatever triggers their imagination. For example,

> Design is much more wide open. I think it's up to you as a designer, but you can look at the problem from underneath. In ['academic' subjects] people are not going to look around something that's flat in front of them; they have to look at it and understand it. With an object, you can look at it from all sides and pull things and press other things. I mean this also in a mental sense.

> If once you are given a brief, there tends to be keywords that will trigger off things; you'll think about things that you have seen, that relate to that word, and then you start to draw on those.

> It works its way through like a modelling process. You can go forward or go back, until everything slots in.

Gratification also appears to be holistic. Fulfilment arises from a sense of practical and of creative achievement. There is the fulfilment of being "able to answer the brief as accurately as possible", but there also is a feeling of things being right, of elements 'clicking' together. Respondents offer powerful metaphors for their solutions' holistic nature. For example,

> Fulfilment feels... like being in love. It's like a complete, light feeling. It's like taking off. It's completely physical, from the stomach out. It's a gut feeling. You just know when you've just managed to create an idea.

4.2 *Browsing*

Browsing is a process that designers use to stimulate their imaginations. In fact, browsing can be a useful metaphor to describe the ways in which experience is accessed and restructured. For example, "Often if I have a project I'll go around the library for inspiration, not even for research."

4.3 *The exchange of opinions*

A crucial part of their method is the ability to exchange opinions, compare ideas and discuss issues with peers and others. Respondents indicated a general concern to move outside the problem spaces to look for models that will allow a different conceptualisation of the problem, broadening the scope of approach. For example,

> To be able to read around the subject... get as many points of view as you can... trying to relate them to the problem you've got to solve within the brief.

5. The importance of cultural and academic background

Looking for evidence of the 'historical schism' between the traditional modes of knowledge used by practice-oriented professionals (such as designers) and those used in scholastic work, we found that designers' own backgrounds have crucial bearing. The split between academic and non-academic background is not complete; some designers show considerable familiarity with the scholastic method.

However, a split does exist in the minds of designers -- even those who are more inclined towards academic work. All designers in the sample attributed development of their own craft to an inclination to "spatial awareness", "modelling and making things", or toward graphics and fine arts. While they may feel at ease in a scholastic environment, these respondents felt that such attitudes have a direct influence on the mode of knowledge most easily accessed in their work. Even the most 'academic' exhibited a tendency towards an holistic approach, based on "total experience".

6. Wider issues and theory

The designers in the sample recognised the importance of being aware of wider social and theoretical issues in their work -- both in providing fresh ways to look at problems and in order to consider consequences of their work. Inevitably, there was a theoretical side to their work that they wanted to be aware of fully.

Designers varied in their concerns for society at large. But, even those who declared they have very personal aesthetic concerns said they find looking at psychology, culture and society very useful. The important subjects and issues cited were environmentalism, ethics, psychology, philosophy, and feminism.

7. Designers' relationship with linear and sequential logic

While designers do not appear at all hostile to books in general, there is evidence of a difficulty in integrating the linear and sequential nature of scholastic work into their work.

Designers do not approach scholastic pursuits systematically. They require mediation in order to turn a linear argument on a page into something designers can "live and breathe". Scholastic argument is subjected to a browsing process; the arguments often are restructured, and allowed to "sink in" without note-taking -- then discussed with peers, to cement the knowledge. For example,

> The reason I find it difficult is that I don't think kind of logically; it's sort of like a whirlpool of thoughts, and I guess I can't really express it in a sort of sequential way.

> I don't find it difficult, but it can be complicated. For me one thing leads to another; words can easily lead to images, images can easily lead to 3-D.

> When people study music, you don't start from like the very beginning. I think it is a very abstract way, to represent a frequency of sound by a dot and line. That's a very abstract way for people to begin. When you've progressed, you really understand about semi-tones and tones and the relationship between notes and harmonics -- which is the basic, but it comes later.

> I can remember things about rooms, structures, etc. I am getting there by thinking in structures; it's just the way my memory works.

> It is not necessarily easy to relate gut feel to learning. They are complete opposites: one is a completely irrational instinct, and one is thought out, has no irrationalities.

8. Reactions to IDEAbase

Designers found IDEAbase to be very exciting, in that it appeared to fit into their practices with respect to their knowledge. IDEAbase allows one to browse through a topic or author, or just to play with ideas and words to see what associations they create in one's mind and in the computer. Knowledge this is restructured in a more convenient and palatable form, allowing it to fit into the mental patterns designers use. At the same time, the system allows for the valued and valuable processes of discussion, comparison and interaction with peers. For example,

> If I am doing an essay on a subject, you just need one word to trigger off ideas. I think [IDEAbase] ... has potential for you not to get stuck into one way of thinking....

The human element in use of a system such as IDEAbase remains very important, especially for designers, given the centrality of human beings to their work. Designers thus express a concern that they be able to suggest and set up semantic correspondences of their own, as well as have access to the authors of the various documents (to follow up ideas). This concern actually is prevalent, and must be addressed in development of the final product. For example, "Computers have the potential for shrinking people's imagination, but they have a potential in education", and "Having contact with people helps, I'd like to be able to meet the person who wrote it."

Reactions to the Buckminster Fuller document depended in part to the familiarity with and interest in the work of Buckminster Fuller. Regardless of respondents' affinity with the work, though, it is possible to draw some overall conclusions. The system is very accessible and within minutes all respondents were able to use it and follow up their own train of thought, regardless of their degree of "computer friendliness". For example, "It took me two seconds to get to the geodesic spheres. It looks more accessible than a typed-up, thick book."

IDEAbase was well received by designers in our sample, provided that it was seen to fit into its "proper" place as a tool and an aid to research, allowing access to more data and information than is possible with books (following different patterns, in an intuitive and playful manner). For example,

> Personally, it would have its place; I wouldn't like to rely on this box. I want to be able to go out and read books and read those, do some interacting yourself with the computer, try and fit it in with what I am doing.

Respondents discriminated at the point where the computer was seen as taking over from humans (attempting to do away with books or imposing its own truths).

9. The concepts of mapping and abduction

From our discussion of the way designers relate to problem-solving and work method, it appears that the concepts of mapping and abduction on which IDEAbase is based are particularly salient and relevant. The concept of mapping is akin to the browsing and structuring of knowledge that designers use in everyday experience but find complex to apply to scholastic work. In fact, often the word *mapping* was used spontaneously by respondents in relation to the sort of mental structures they create when researching a subject. For example,

> There probably is a good link [between linear argument and design] but I am not in that path. If you could apply mapping to essays, etcetera, I'd probably remember them better.

Abduction also rang true to designers, who strive to look at problems from all angles (applying different points of view and paradigms to organise the problem space).

10. Conclusions

IDEAbase could have a place in designers' work, helping them to research design-related issues and theories. For example, "I am sure it could help my research. Victor Papanek has a system similar to it. I think it's good."

The strengths of IDEAbase come from the way in which

knowledge is accessed and structured, which closely matches designers' own ways of working. Given designers' laborious way of mediating scholastic work and integrating it in the total experience they draw upon, IDEAbase can widen the scope of designers' work and free those who are less academically gifted from the tyranny of linear and sequential argument (while benefiting from its insight).

5

Mapping spatial cognition with computers

PHIL MOOSE, TERI STUELAND, KRISTA KERN AND TOM GENTRY

Center for Telecommunications Courses, California State University, Stanislaus, Turlock, CA 95382 USA
moose%ctc.csustan.edu@altair.csustan.edu

Abstract. In this chapter, fractal geometry, digital video technology and research regarding spatial cognition are combined to create new methods for describing mental models. Pointing behaviours recorded on videotape, and digitised sketch maps, provide general purpose means to derive quantitative measures for the study of cognitive maps. Fractal dimension (D) estimates of cognitive maps were computed to study individual differences, and the dynamic properties of mental models.

Estimates of D for cognitive maps were found to be sensitive to an apparent asymmetry of spatial processes, but to exhibit low correlations with tests of personality and intelligence. Results suggest that the type of "imagination" used in cognitive maps may not be assessed effectively by the principal factors common to psychometric measures of cognition.

1. Introduction

1.1 *The applications of fractal geometry*

In the relatively brief period since the terms "fractal" and "fractal dimension" were coined by Mandelbrot (1975), a rapidly expanding literature has emerged utilising these concepts to describe natural phenomena. Schroeder (1991) provides a readable account of the ubiquitous applications for this mathematics, including several uses associated with human behaviour. The National Research Council's recommendations (Steen, 1990) for "new approaches to numeracy" begin with a chapter which introduces the fractal dimension concept. And, the Peitgen, Jurgens, and Saupe (1992a, 1992b) textbooks *Fractals for the Classroom* -- commissioned by the National Council of Teachers of Mathematics -- are designed for general education uses, beginning in high school.

This broad-based dissemination of fractal geometry can be attributed to the availability of increasingly affordable computing machines and the improved fit between natural forms and these quantitative methods. Sarraille & Gentry (1994) review scientific journal databases with respect to fractal-related applications across disciplines; they note that fractal dimension measures are confined largely to the "physical" sciences. However, this may be more a matter of the words used, since power law functions have a long history in behavioural and social research. Gentry (1994) suggests that psychologists can re-interpret this literature whereby the exponents derived from log/log plots now can be viewed as descriptions of cognitive complexity. Abraham, Abraham, & Shaw (1990) and Goertzel (1993a, 1993b) provide substantial agendas for the application of nonlinear analysis -- including fractal geometry -- for many areas of interest to students of humanity.

This chapter focuses on techniques being used in a research program seeking to characterise the geometry of human imagination (Gentry, Goodman, Wakefield & Wright, 1986; Gentry & Wakefield, 1991; Gentry, 1991; Moose, 1991; Kern, 1991, 1992; Sarraille & Gentry, 1994; Stueland, 1994). We utilise two behaviours humans use to communicate spatial information: pointing and sketching. Although our primary interest is to generate accessible representations of individual cognitive maps, these behaviours also are relevant to some computer-human interaction (CHI).

The working hypothesis that guides our experiments is that the computation of fractal dimensions may be similar to the process applied by the brain in discriminating features that are contained in data streams arriving from the senses. Baldly stated, if the geometry of nature is fractal -- as suggested by Mandelbrot (1975, 1977, 1982) -- then our cognitive maps also may be fractal. What's more, the fractal concepts may support a long standing suggestion that Euclidean geometry is not a satisfactory mathematics for describing human visual perception.

1.2 *Fractal aspects of human visual perception*

The proposition that visual perception is inherently non-Euclidean was made explicit by Luneberg (1947; see also Blank, 1959) and was supported subsequently by empirical results from a variety of studies (Dodwell, 1982). Despite evidence that a principle sensory input to the brain -- vision -- is inappropriately described with the geometry of Euclid, there were few options until the introduction of fractal geometry.

Earlier approaches which did allow for non-Euclidean methods include the multi-dimensional scaling (MDS) algorithms derived from the paper by Abelson & Tukey (1963) and extended by Kruskal (1964a, 1964b) and Shepard (1966). Despite several problems with MDS techniques (detailed by Shepard (1974)), this mathematics provided the starting point for the present research; it used the KYST-2A software (Kruskal, Young, & Seery, 1977) in initial analysis of the pointing procedures described below.

A primary objective in Gentry & Wakefield (1991) was to compare MDS methods with the newer fractal geometry approach. It was suggested that the fractal approach is better in characterising the dynamics of and individual differences in cognitive maps. In short, Gentry & Wakefield hypothesise that cognitive maps are fractal.

2. Background

2.1 *Cognitive maps*

The meaning of "cognitive maps" is the topic of long term debate in psychology; the use of these terms by CHI researchers has expanded the range of interested participants. Both "cognitive" and "maps" elicit a diversity of interpretations and disputes. For example, Downs and Stea (1977) define cognitive mapping as "an abstraction covering those cognitive or mental abilities that enable us to collect, organise, store, recall and manipulate information about the spatial environment." Although we shall review some of the interpretations of "cognitive map" briefly, our objective in this chapter is to describe some practical methods for studying human behaviours relevant to interactions with computers.

Laszlo & Masulli (1993) begin a conference proceedings on this topic with

> Our use of the term 'cognitive maps' refers to the process by which an organism makes representations of its environment in its brain, an activity which most contemporary brain scientists seem to agree is one of the brain's main functions. This idea, in various forms, can be traced back to Hippocrates.

The same collection ends with Eco's (1993) observation that

> ... this conference is about the problem of maps, and who better than a student of semiotics or linguistics problems in general can be aware of the fact that the universe is a *confederation of different maps* [emphasis added], each of them representing the world in a differ-

ent way? The problem today is whether these maps are commensurable, comparable, translatable among themselves, and whether there exists a metalanguage which will enable them to be described even when they are contradictory ....

(pp. 281-2)

One working assumption of the research summarised here is that a new "metalanguage" is available to translate among Eco's "confederation of different maps". This metalanguage arises from a cognitive change in our bedrock beliefs about the concepts of "dimension" and of "space" itself. The advent of fractal geometry is more than a new mathematical tool to describe the natural world better, although it is proving to be very useful in that regard. Its more fundamental contribution is that the concept of fractal dimension has begun to revise our thinking about the very fabric of experience per se -- what gestalt psychologists called the "ground," but which is more commonly labelled the nature of "extent" or "space."

Elsewhere (Gentry & Wakefield, 1991; Gentry, 1994), we have traced the arguments from Mach (1886) to Jaynes (1976) that individuals' sense of "space" is the point of departure for all conscious awareness -- and that with new ideas about "space", we are confronted with potential changes in how we think about everything.

Mandelbrot's (1975, 1977, 1982) introduction of the formalisms needed to think in terms of "fractional dimensions" and "fractals" has broken the mindset that dimensionality comes in whole integer units. We now can think in terms of measuring spatial complexities to any degree of precision warranted by the available techniques. It has become possible to detect subtle differences in human abilities and behaviours with a precision not available using previous methods.

For example, Westheimer (1991) reported that the classical "just noticeable difference" threshold for changes in the fractal dimension of an irregular contour can be measured in the few parts per thousand range. He found that his observers could discriminate a change as small as 0.0085 in a contour with a starting fractal dimension of $D = 1.15$. In practical terms, for people developing artificial visual systems, this provides benchmark estimates for the sensitivity needed in a system in order to equal or exceed the discrimination capacity of humans to detect changes in complex visual tasks. Our work suggests that similar sensitivities can be achieved using the fractal dimension to characterise motor behaviours that reflect cognitive maps.

Edward Toleman (1948) was one of the first experimenters to investigate and publish about cognitive mapping. In his research, he observed the ability of rats to get from a starting position to a goal by a route never used before. Toleman first trained rats in a maze with a path that took the animals in a direction opposite from the goal. In the test situation, the rats were confronted with a fan of maze arms, such that the frequency of the initial direction selected would indicate whether or not the rat had merely learned a serial sequence of stimulus-response behaviours (or actually had formed a generalised cognitive map, so that it could choose the general direction to the goal).

Toleman's results (Downs and Stea, 1977, pp. 31-36; Toleman, 1948) support the view that organisms such as rats can develop cognitive maps that enable them to take novel routes to previously visited geographic locations. This type of internal environmental model now is considered common to many species. However, debates over how this is accomplished continue (Alcock, 1989; Ellen & Thinus-Blanc, 1987; Lieblich, 1982; McFarland, 1985; Olton, 1982).

Cognitive maps may entail abstract representations of real environmental spaces. Some of our work in developing geographic information systems (GIS) has been directed towards such constants (Gentry & Wakefield, 1991). However, our studies also have included the mapping of "people" and "things", with the goal of deriving nonlinear geometric models for general cognition. Exploring what we mean by "imagination" provides the focus for our research.

Some investigators make distinctions between mental maps based on perception versus those based on cognition (e.g., Bedford, 1993). Carley & Palmquist (1992) utilise a linguistic analysis approach to construct maps, by applying computer assisted analysis of spoken and textual comparisons of terms, concepts and information structures. Other uses of the term "mapping" appear in the development of software to support decision analysis (Zhang, Chen, & Bezdek, 1989), in neural networks intended to aid or simulate cognition (Eberts, Villegas, Phillips & Eberts, 1992; Holyoak & Thagard, 1989) and in the transfer of training from one computer command structure to another (Schumacher & Gentner, 1988; Schmidt, Fischer, Heydemann & Hoffmann, 1991).

The expanding diversity of meanings for cognitive or mental maps makes Eco's concerns a central agenda for those interested in "computerised tools as intermediaries in the communication of mental maps." A common spatial language and a quantitative system for describing "maps" of all types may remain only an ideal, but the emergence of fractal geometry is a new opportunity for developing a unified theory of spatial cognition and associated technologies.

2.2 *Fractal geometry and space*

It is likely that many readers know of Mandelbrot's contributions, due to the elaborate computer graphics associated with the set named after him. Creating complex images via iteration of small equations (such as the Mandelbrot set) has become a popular "screen-saving" technique.

Mandelbrot was explicit in his claim that the concept of a "fractal dimension" represents an improvement both in our understanding of "dimension" and in the significance of the observer in anything -- even mathematics! The significance of the observer has been most distasteful for some, since it continues a theme which opened the 20th Century with the birth of relativistic physics. On the first point, Mandelbrot (1982, p. 12) states that "the loose notion of dimension splits into several distinct components"; on the latter, he describes his notion of "effective dimension" as

> the relation between mathematical sets and natural objects.... In other words, effective dimension inevitably has a subjective basis. It is a matter of approximation and therefore of degree of resolution.

(p. 17).

Using iterated equations to generate patterns that model natural phenomena is increasingly popular in the field of computer graphics, but it is running this process in reverse that provides the significant achievement which makes fractal geometry a powerful analytical method. Barnsley (1988) provides a good introduction to the methods by which it is possible to go from images of complex forms to numbers that characterise the fractal dimensionality of natural patterns. Barnsley (1988, p. 3) defines the

> fractal dimension of a set [as] a number which tells how densely the set occupies the metric space in which it lies. It is invariant under various streachings [sic] and squeezings of the underlying space. This makes the fractal dimension meaningful as an experimental observable; it possesses a certain robustness, and is independent of the measurement units.

We use the term fractal dimension (D) to denote what is more formally called the "capacity" or Hausdorff dimension. Our computations of D which utilised the Sarraille-DiFalco computer program also provide "correlation" and "information" dimension estimates, but in this research they have been essentially the same as the capacity dimensions. The potential utility for different types of fractal dimension calculations is described by Schroeder (1991).

2.3 *Pointing behaviour as data*

The antiquity of using pointing arms and fingers to convey information is necessarily speculative, but it is not difficult to believe that it predates both the emergence of writing (about 6,000 years before the present, "ybp") and symbolic drawings (about 30,000 ybp). If one considers the many examples of non-human intraspecies communication involving the orientation of body parts, pointing must have been one of the original geographic information systems used by our ancestors. Indeed, it still is commonly used whenever the auditory language channel is inappropriate -- such as in noisy environments, or where silence is important.

The ability of humans to point in the direction of real or imagined targets has been employed in several types of research on spatial abilities. Clinical uses of pointing have been reported since the middle of the 19th Century (von Graefe, 1854), and remain common tests for a range of neurological disorders (e.g., Riddoch, 1917; Bock & Kommerel, 1986). Ott, Eckmiller, and Bock (1987) constructed a head-mounted, computer-controlled device to record pointing towards 80 light emitting diodes contained within the head gear. The subjects could not see their pointing behaviour (which is important for clinical testing).

In treatment of autistic children, pointing behaviours have been used to replace "autistic leading" and as an intermediary step in the acquisition of verbal behaviour (Carr & Kemp, 1989). These clinical studies and the use of pointing behaviours to improve autistic dysfunctions are consistent with the view that pointing represents a very early manifestation of an individual's cognitive mapping abilities.

As with all gross motor movements, in addressing pointing behaviour the researcher is confronted with the problem of response specification and measurement. The literature contains a range of methods that vary in complexity, cost and precision. Duhamel, Pinek, & Brouchon (1986) measured pointing towards auditory targets with blindfolded subjects by rating whether the index finger of the pointing hand was either to the left or right of a sound source. Using this relatively simple and inexpensive method, they found significant differences between left-versus right-handed subjects (right handers were more accurate) and between which arm/hand was used, irrespective of handedness (left hand/arms were more accurate).

Presson, Delange, and Hazelrigg (1989) devised a hand-held circular dial with a pointer that could be moved by subjects to indicate directions, for experiments on spatial memory of maps and paths. Their objective was to determine the effects of scale. They found that small scale displays were coded in an orientation specific way, while very large scale displays were remembered "in a more orientation-free manner." They cited their work as support for the

> view that there are distinct spatial representations, one more perceptual and episodic and one more integrated and model-like, that have developed to meet different demands faced by mobile organisms.

The advent of the microcomputer has brought pointing devices that offer new opportunities for the assessment of individual differences in spatial abilities. Jones (1989) has used mouse, joystick, and track ball to manipulate the cursor in studies where subjects "point" to targets displayed on the screen. He found that estimates of processing rates (bits/sec.) based on Fitts' method were substantially slower for the computer pointing tasks than for problems of similar difficulty measured with direct pointing (Fitts 1954, Fitts & Peterson, 1964; see also Langolf, Chaffin, & Foulke, 1976).

Sholl (1987) used a modified joystick in a "point-to-un-seen-targets" test of cognitive maps for geographic regions of different size. Her results suggest that the orientation of schemata directs user orientation with respect to local environments, but that orientation with respect to large geographical regions is supported by a different type of cognitive structure. This finding is similar to that in the study by Presson, Delange, and Hazelrigg (1989) cited above.

Gentry and Wakefield (1991) review the literature on using pointing as a behavioural measure, and describe a procedure for characterising cognitive maps using pointing behaviour recorded on videotape. These recordings are processed to create composite plots of the subject's pointing motions toward imagined targets. The resulting "cloud-of-points" (COP) plots are used to compute the fractal dimensions of the subject's cognitive map. The present experiments were conducted to provide a more extensive examination of the method described by Gentry & Wakefield.

2.4 *Sketch maps as data*

The step from (a) pointing with a finger in order to indicate features in the environment to (b) drawing a representative sketch in the dirt may not seem a particularly dramatic advance in cognitive abilities, since we combine the two easily when communicating with each other. But a good deal of experimental evidence suggests that the sketch map is a much more complex task, and has greater sensitivity to experiential variables and individual differences.

Evans (1980) reviewed the use of sketch map methodologies that show the effects of age, gender, culture, and type of environment. Reports of gender differences in cognition generally attract attention; sketch maps have been used in several such experiments (Boardman, 1990; Grieve & Van Staden, 1988; Holding & Holding, 1989; Pearce, 1977). In general, sex differences appear to be related more to what is emphasised or to style. Also, such differences are not apparent in younger children.

Sketch maps are sensitive particularly to age, therefore are used in developmental studies (Biel, 1986; Blades, 1990; Golledge, 1985; Grieve & Van Staden, 1988). Other variables that are said to influence the construction of sketch maps include (a) spatial abilities, as measured by some psychometric tests (Moore, 1975), and (b) measures of visualisation, orientation, and sense of direction (Rovine & Weisman, 1989).

The report by Blades (1990) concerning the reliability of data collected from sketch maps is central to the analysis method described in this chapter. Blades utilised the common "two independent judges" method to obtain reliability estimates. But the work of Lewin & Wakefield (1979) and Wakefield (1980) demonstrated that an unexpectedly high concordance between observers is needed to achieve significant correlations. For example, if two observers detected 90 percent of the target features in a task and their inter-observer agreement were 82 percent, a zero ($r = 0.00$) correlation would result!

The use of trained observers or "experts" to render independent scores, which then are used to compute the reliability of a measurement, is applied in many areas involving complex patterns (such as human hand writing or sketching). Computing fractal dimensions for these types of patterns offers new quantitative methods in the analysis of human cognitive complexity.

3. Method

We present here new methods for studying the complexity of mental maps -- methods that are very sensitive to the fractional dimensionality of spatial cognition. Our intention is to describe the methodologies that we have developed. These techniques may have general utility for a range of research interests that involve the analysis of motor behaviours recorded on videotape, or that involve hand movements and drawings.

Two different groups of subjects were used. The first group provided data for (a) manual computation of the capacity fractal dimension of pointing behaviours and (b) an automated analysis of sketch maps. The second experimental group provided data for a replication of the pointing behaviour results, using a more automated videotape analysis system and a fast algorithm (fd3) for computing capacity, information, and correlation dimensions (Sarraille, 1991).

(Copies of the fd3 program for Unix and DOS, plus related documentation, are available. Contact *john%ishi.csustan.edu@altair.csustan.edu.*)

3.1 *Pointing Experiment 1*

SUBJECTS

The subjects were 55 university students (35 female, 20 male) enrolled in an introductory psychology course; they received extra credit for participating. Their ages ranged from 17 to 37, with a mean of 21. Each participant completed a consent form describing the nature of the experiment and was told that all information would remain confidential. Confidentiality was assured by assigning a code number to each participant.

QUESTIONNAIRES

Three pencil and paper tests were administered during three regular class periods: Eysenck's (1975) personality questionnaire (EPQ), two parts of the Differential Aptitude Test (DAT), and a test of spatial relations and verbal reasoning (Bennett, Seashore, & Wesman, 1984).

APPARATUS

A video camcorder recorded subjects' pointing behaviour during the individual sessions, in a windowless room. A meter stick was placed on the wall directly behind the subjects, to provide a reference scale.

Two audio cassette players were used to provide continuous prerecorded instructions. (Five audio instruction tapes had been created prior to the experiment. The first tape explained what would transpire during the session. The four remaining audio tapes contained 20 randomised landmark locations, used to elicit pointing responses.)

The videotapes of subjects were analysed using a VCR, a 33-cm (13-inch) colour television monitor, and a 23 x 28-cm (8 x 11-inch) piece of plexiglass. Acetate sheets (also 23 x 28-cm) and black, water resistant pens were used to record pointing locations on the plexiglass overlays.

PROCEDURE

Prior to videotaping, a series of steps was initiated. First, during a regular class period (conducted in a windowless room), all subjects were instructed to draw a sketch map of the campus -- a map that included nineteen specific landmarks. Then subjects were directed to go outside the building and stand facing in a direction which made all target landmarks visible. Verbal instructions were given to look over the campus and to create a mental picture of the surroundings and the locations of specified landmarks. Subjects then were asked to point to these landmarks as each one was verbalised. Following this direct observation of target landmarks, subjects returned immediately to the classroom and were instructed to draw a second sketch map.

Next, subjects were taken one at a time into a windowless room. Masking tape on the floor directly across from the camcorder showed subjects where to stand. A ping-pong ball, drilled to make a finger-sized hole, was given to each subject so that it could be placed on the forefinger of their right (R) or left (L) hands. An L-R-R-L or R-L-L-R control pattern was used alternately across subjects, in an effort to counterbalance any order effects due to which arm was used first for pointing. The ping-pong ball made pointing locations easier to identify later, when researchers analysed videotapes.

The video camcorder was stopped after the first and third audio tapes were completed. This provided time for subjects to change the ping pong ball from one hand to the other.

Prior to the start of a session, all subjects listened to a prerecorded tape with the following instructions:

> During the entire procedure, please keep your eyes closed and try to relax as best you can. When I instruct you to point to a specific location please hold your hand steady until I say okay. Let's begin. Imagine yourself on the front steps of the classroom building. You will be facing Monte Vista Avenue. The reflecting pond and fountain will also be in front of you.

The imagined geographic location was identical to the site where subjects had stood during the earlier practice session. It should be noted that when subjects were in the room used for the videotape session, they were at a 90 degree angle to the imagined location. Consequently, subjects had the task of imagining themselves rotated to a geographic orientation orthogonal to where they were standing during the actual testing procedure.

The behaviour of importance in this task was the subjects' ability to point toward specified campus landmarks, viewed from an imagined position. This behaviour was recorded on videotape and used to extract estimates of the fractal dimension (D) for pointing to these targets.

DATA REDUCTION AND ANALYSIS

After all subjects were videotaped, the tapes were played in a VCR; each subject's pointing locations were plotted on 23 x 28-cm acetate sheets. Each sheet was taped onto the plexiglass, which had been attached to a television monitor. The plexiglass provided a flat surface on which to mark the pointing locations. Each subject yielded two acetates, one for right hand pointing locations and one for the left hand. The cloud-of-points (COP) data from each subject were analysed by making 15 copies of the COP patterns. The copies were used to circle the cloud-of-points according to the procedure described by Barnsley (1988, p. 190).

The circle templates were overlaid one copy at a time, starting with the largest radius and ranging to the smallest. In all, 15 circles were used, with radii ranging from 6 mm (1/4 inch) to 88.9 mm (3-1/2 inches). The "algorithm" used was a procedure whose aim was to cover all points with a minimal number of circles of each radius. No circle was counted that did not include a data point. This procedure was performed for the 15 circles, and data were plotted as a power function. A fractal dimension was computed for each cloud-of-points set. (The logarithm of the number of circles needed to cover the points with a particular radius was plotted against the logarithm of the reciprocal of the radius for the corresponding circle. A regression line was computed through the resulting points, using the 04-StatWorks program for the Macintosh. The slope of the regression line was the estimate of the fractal dimension. This particular estimate is known as the capacity dimension; an example using cloud-of-points can be found in Barnsley (1988, p. 190)).

RESULTS

Only two significant correlations were observed between pointing behaviours and subjects' psychometric test scores. The correlations between the left arm and the DAT verbal subtest was $r = 0.309$ ($p = 0.022$); the DAT spatial subtest was $r = 0.276$ ($p = 0.044$). All other correlations were smaller -- and nonsignificant. The principle result in this pointing experiment and in the following second experiment was the difference in fractal dimensions of the cloud-of-points generated by the left versus right arms (Table 1).

Table 1. Paired t-test between estimated fractal dimensions (D) of subject's right versus left arm COP

	Left Arm	Right Arm
Mean	0.984	0.952
SD	0.078	0.082

Notes: t = 4.118; df = 54; p < 0.001.

3.2 *Sketch map analysis and results*

The sketch maps described in the method section were used to compare estimates of fractal dimension, between the drawings made before subjects viewed campus landmarks to those made after they had returned to the classroom. The drawings were converted to "islands" by connecting landmarks with straight lines, specifying that connecting lines could not intersect. This method yielded an irregular perimeter polygon for each drawing. The resulting outlined sketch maps then were digitised using a Targa8 framegrabber and a microcomputer running Jandel Scientific's JAVA image analysis program. The edge tracking feature of JAVA yielded x,y coordinates for the perimeter of sketch map "islands." The data then were analysed by applying the DiFalco-Sarraille algorithm to compute D.

A t-test between D values derived from the first sketch maps and those for the second set indicated that the brief direct observation of landmarks resulted in a significant increase in the fractal dimension of the post-observation drawings, as indicated in Table 2.

One also might ask how the two methods correlated in terms of the fractal dimension of internal cognitive maps (i.e., D derived from sketch maps versus D derived from pointing behaviour). These correlations are shown in Table 3.

Table 2. Paired t-test between estimated fractal dimensions (D) of the pre-observation versus post-observation sketch maps

	Pre-observation D	Post-observation D
Mean	1.177	1.212
SD	0.072	0.075

Note: t = 2.905; df = 53; p < 0.005.

Table 3. Correlations between fractal dimension estimates (D) for the sketch maps versus pointing methods

	D (Pre-sketch)	D (Post-sketch)	D Left Arm	D Right Arm
Pre-sketch D	1.000	0.255	0.231	0.162
Post-sketch D		1.000	0.046	- 0.006
Left Arm D			1.000	0.745*
Right Arm D				1.000

Note: *p < 0.001.

The only significant correlation was between the two arms in the pointing procedure (r = 0.745, p < .001). Even though pointing with the left arm exhibited significantly higher values of D, the fractal dimensions of the cloud-of-points for the two arms in the same individual were highly correlated. The correlations in Table 3 suggest that sketch maps involve a cognitive process that is sufficiently different from pointing behaviour to warrant separate consideration.

At this juncture, it was decided to focus on the asymmetry in pointing behaviour, since it was difficult to believe that such a small effect could reach the p < 0.001 level of significance. Work by Westheimer (1991) had been consistent with Barnsley's (1988) claims for fractal dimension sensitivity, so we conducted a second pointing experiment to test the robustness of our initial main effect. The subjects were different, the experimenter was different, and the operative elements were a very different mixture of people, places and things. The pyschometric battery was expanded and the video analysis method was changed from the manual overlays and hand drawn circles to a rear projection digitising tablet that yielded pointing.

3.3 *Pointing Experiment 2*

SUBJECTS

Subjects for the second pointing experiment consisted of 42 university students (13 males and 29 females) enrolled in an introductory psychology class. The mean age of males and females was 20.08 and 20.48 years, respectively.

QUESTIONNAIRES

Subjects completed four psychometric tests: the Minnesota Multiphasic Personality Inventory-2 (MMPI-2; Hathaway & McKinley, 1989), the Eysenck Personality Questionnaire (EPQ; Eysenck, 1975), and two sections of the Differential Aptitude Tests (DAT) -- verbal reasoning and spatial relations (Bennett, Seashore, & Wesman, 1984).

The EPQ and the two sections of the DAT were administered during regular class periods. Due to the large amount of time required to complete the MMPI-2, this measure was given as a homework assignment.

APPARATUS

Again, a video camera recorded pointing behaviours in a windowless room. Masking tape on the floor indicated where subjects were to stand. As before, a ping-pong ball with a hole drilled in it was placed on the forefinger of each subject to facilitate analysis of the videotaped pointing behaviours.

PROCEDURE

Two video recording sessions were conducted. During Session 1, subjects first pointed to all targets using their right hands. Then they were asked to point toward the same targets using their left hands. The subjects pointed first with their left hands in the second session.

STIMULUS MATERIALS

Two audio tapes, one for each pointing session, provided instructions for the participants. The directions were as follows:

> During the entire procedure, please relax and try to keep your eyes closed. When I instruct you to point to a specific person, location, or object, please point and hold your arm steady until I say 'okay.' You can hold your arm as close to or far from your body as you like, but please hold your arm steady until I say 'okay.' Let's begin.

After providing these procedural instructions, the audio tapes gave a list of targets to which subjects were to point. During each session, the names of 18 cities, 18 people, and 18 common objects were given. The tapes allowed 10 seconds for each subject to imagine the target and then to decide where to point. The order of targets remained the same across subjects and between sessions.

DATA REDUCTION AND ANALYSIS

Videotapes of the pointing behaviours were analysed by using the computer program SigmaScan (Jandel Scientific, 1991). The projected videotaped images were reflected off of a mirror under a rear projection digitising glass tablet. A mouse with gun-sight cross-hairs was used to mark target locations that had been indicated by subjects. The program then recorded the x,y coordinates of data points onto a spreadsheet. The fractal dimension of the coordinates was computed by using the fd3 program. Separate fractal dimensions were calculated for each of the three kinds of targets. Correlations were computed (using SPSS) between (a) fractal dimensions of pointing toward people, locations, and objects and (b) scores on the MMPI-2, EPQ, and DAT.

RESULTS

A 2x3 factorial ANOVA was calculated to determine whether either (a) the hand with which subjects pointed or (b) the type of target significantly affected fractal dimensions of the pointing behaviours. A significant main effect was found for the hand used: $F (1, 246) = 12.671$, $p < .001$. The fractal dimension of pointing with the left hand ($M = 0.998$, $SD = 0.143$) was significantly higher than that for the right hand ($M = 0.899$, $SD = 0.156$).

The type of target toward which subjects pointed (people, locations, or objects) had no significant main effect, $p > .4$. Also, no significant interaction was found between the hand used for pointing and the type of target, $p > .8$.

Correlation coefficients also were calculated between (a) fractal dimensions for pointing toward various targets and (b) scores on the psychometric tests. No significant correlations were found.

4. Discussion

The major findings of this research suggest that the pointing behaviour used to study cognitive maps is consistent with conclusions of the literature on asymmetry of human brain function. Namely, the dimensionality of pointing with the left hand/arm motor system is greater than that for pointing with the right arm, as measured by the fractal dimension. This is consistent with the results of Duhamel, Pinek, & Brouchon (1986), which showed that the accuracy for auditory localisation was better for the left arm (irrespective of "handedness"). It also is consistent with findings that so called "split brain" right handed subjects whose corpus callosum has been severed render more realistic drawings with their left hands (Ornstein, 1985, p. 153).

The failure to find any consistent relationships between the psychometric tests and the apparently robust pointing

asymmetry supports a growing suspicion that some important forms of cognition are not assessed with commonly used psychometric tests.

The work of West (1991, 1992a, 1992b) describes the experiences of visual thinkers and gifted people with learning difficulties as some of "the ironies of creativity". It suggests that spatial behaviour studied in our experiments may be understood better in the context of psychometric measures that reflect the "imagination" used in pointing towards imagined targets.

We noted in the introduction that multidimensional scaling methods developed by Shepard, Kruskal and others had been used in initial analysis of distance measures derived from the pointing behaviours reported in Gentry & Wakefield (1991). Shepard (1987) has described a "probabilistic geometry" for generalisation in learning that includes exponential decay functions. This may resolve his earlier concerns (Shepard, 1974) about the MDS methods, and may be compatible with the proposition that power functions (e.g., fractal dimensions) are appropriate, robust, and sensitive measures of the dynamics of human behaviour and cognition.

Acknowledgments

The authors are especially indebted to the long term encouragement and support provided by Frederick Abraham, James Goodwin, Sally Goerner, Julie Gorman, John Sarraille, and James Wakefield.

References

ABELSON, R.P. & TUKEY, J.W. 1963, Efficient utilization of nonnumerical information in quantitative analysis: general theory and the case of simple order. *Annals of Mathematical Statistics* 34, 1347-1369.

ABRAHAM, F.D., ABRAHAM, R.H. & SHAW, C.D. 1990, *A Visual Introduction to Dynamical Systems Theory for Psychology.* (Aerial Press, Santa Cruz, CA).

ALCOCK, J. 1989, *Animal Behavior: An Evolutionary Approach*, 4th ed. (Sinauer Associates, Sunderland, MA).

BARNSLEY, M.F. 1988, *Fractals Everywhere* (Academic Press, New York).

BEDFORD, F.L. 1993, Perceptual and cognitive spatial learning. *Journal of Experimental Psychology: Human Perception & Performance* **19**, 517-530.

BENNETT, G.K., SEASHORE, H.G., & WESMAN, A.G. 1984, *Differential Aptitude Tests: Technical Supplement* (Psychological Corporation, San Antonio, TX).

BIEL, A. 1986, Children's spatial knowledge of their home environment. *Children's Environments Quarterly* **3**, 2-9.

BIEL, A. & TORELL, G. 1982, Experience as a determinant of children's neighbourhood knowledge. *Goteborg Psychological Reports* **12**, 21.

BLADES, M. 1990, The reliability of data collected from sketch maps. *Journal of Environmental Psychology* **10**, 327-339.

BLANK, A.A. 1959, The Lunbeberg theory of binocular space perception. In S. Koch (ed), *Psychology: A Study of a Science, Volume 1. Sensory, Perceptual and Physiological Formulations.* (McGraw-Hill, New York).

BOCK, O. & KOMMERELL, G. 1986, Visual localization after strabismus surgery is compatible with the "outflow" theory. *Vision Research* **26**, 1825-1829.

BOARDMAN, D. 1990, Graphicacy revisited: mapping abilities and gender differences. *Educational Review* **42**, 57-64.

CARLEY, K. & PALMQUIST, M.E. 1992, Extracting, representing, and analyzing mental models. *Social Forces* **70**(3), 601-636.

CARR, E.G. & KEMP, D.C. 1989, Functional equivalence of autistic leading and communicative pointing: Analysis and treatment. *Journal of Autism and Developmental Disorders* **19**, 561-578.

DIFALCO, P. 1991, A new program for computing the fractal dimension of a 'cloud of points.' Paper presented to the Inaugural Conference for the Society for Chaos Theory in Psychology, San Francisco, August 15-16.

DODWELL, P.C. 1982, Geometrical approaches to visual processing. In D.J. Ingle, M.A. Goodale, & R.J.W. Mansfield (eds), *Analysis of Visual Behavior* (MIT Press, Cambridge, MA).

DOWNS, R.M., & STEA, D. 1977, *Maps in Mind: Reflections on Cognitive Mapping* (Harper Row, New York).

DUHAMEL, J-R., PINEK, B., & BROUCHON, M. 1986, Manual pointing to auditory targets: performances of right versus left handed subjects. *Cortex* **22**, 633-638.

EBERTS, R., VILLEGAS, L., PHILLIPS, C. & EBERTS, C. 1992, Using neural net modeling for user assistance in HCI tasks. Special issue: applications of cognitive theory and science to human-computer interaction: I. *International Journal of Human-Computer Interaction* **4**, 59-77.

EYSENCK, H.J. 1975, Eysenck Personality Questionnaire. Educational and Industrial Testing Service, San Diego, CA.

ECO, U. 1993). Commentary. In E. Laszlo & I. Masulli (eds), *The Evolution of Cognitive Maps.* (Gordon & Breach, Amsterdam).

ELLEN, P. & THINUS-BLANC, C. 1987, Cognitive processes and spatial orientation in animal and man. *Proceedings of the NATO Advanced Study Institute on Cognitive Processes and Spatial Orientation in Animal and Man* (La Baume-les-Aix, France, 1985)(Kluwer Academic Publishers, Dordrecht.

EVANS, G.W. 1980, Environmental cognition. *Psychological Bulletin* **88**, 259-287.

FITTS, P.M. 1954, The information capacity of the human motor system in controlling the amplitude of human movement. *Journal of Experimental Psychology* **47**, 381-391.

FITTS, P.M. & PETERSON, J.R. 1964, Information capacity of discrete motor responses. *Journal of Experimental Psychology* **67**, 103-112.

GENTRY, T.A., GOODMAN, N., WAKEFIELD, J.A. JR., AND WRIGHT, R.R. 1986, Geometric properties of individual human image spaces. Paper presented to the 10th American Imagery Conference, San Francisco, California.

GENTRY, T.A. & WAKEFIELD, J.A. JR. 1991, Methods for measuring spatial cognition. In D.M. Mark & A.U. Frank (eds), *Proceedings: NATO Advanced Study Institute on the Cognitive & Linguistic Aspects of Geographic Space* (Kluwer Academic Publishers, Dordrecht).

GENTRY, T.A. 1991, From Fechner to fractals. *The Psychology Teacher Network* **1**(2), 5-11(The American Psychological Assn., Washington).

GENTRY, T.A. 1994, Fractal geometry and human understanding. In A. Gilgen & F. Abraham (eds), *Chaos Theory in Psychology* (Greenwood, Westport, CT)(in press).

GOERTZEL, B. 1993a, *The Structure of Intelligence* (Springer-Verlag, New York).

GOERTZEL, B. 1993b, *The Evolving Mind* (Gordon & Breach, Langhorne, PA).

GOLLEDGE, R.G. 1985, A conceptual model and empirical analysis of children's acquisition of spatial knowledge. *Journal of Environmental Psychology* **5**, 125-152.

GRIEVE, K.W. & VAN STADEN, F.J. 1988, A cross-cultural study of children's cognitive maps. *South African Journal of Psychology* **18**, 91-95.

HOLDING, C.S. & HOLDING, D.H. 1989, Acquisition of route network knowledge by males and females. *Journal of General Psychology* **116**(1), 29-41.

HOLYOAK, K.J. & THAGARD, P. 1989, Analogical mapping by constraint satisfaction. *Cognitive Science* **13**, 295-355.

JAYNES, J. 1976, *The Origin of Consciousness in the Breakdown of the Bicameral Mind* (Houghton Mifflin, Boston).

JONES, T. 1989, Psychology of computer use: XVI. Effect of computer-pointing devices on children's processing rate. *Perceptual and Motor Skills* **69**, 1259-1263.

KERN, K. 1991, Using D to search for relationships between a new measure of cognition and individual differences in personality and intelligence. Paper presented to the Inaugural Conference for a Society for Chaos Theory in Psychology, San Francisco, August 15-16.

KERN, K. 1992, The Geometry of Imagination: Using the Fractal Dimension to Search for Relationships between a New Measure of Spatial Cognition and Individual Differences in Personality and Intelligence. Unpublished master's thesis, California State University, Stanislaus, Turlock, CA.

KRUSKAL, J.B. 1964a, Multidimensional scaling by optimizing goodness of fit to a nonmetric hypothesis. *Psychometrika* **29**, 1-27.

KRUSKAL, J.B. 1964b, Nonmetric multidimensional scaling: a numerical method. *Psychometrika* **29**, 1-27.

KRUSKAL, J.B., YOUNG, F.W., & SEERY, J.B. 1977, *How to Use KYST-2A: A Very Flexible Program to Do Multidimensional Scaling and Unfolding* (Bell Laboratories, Murry Hill, NJ).

LANGOLF, G.D., CHAFFIN, D.B., & FOULKE, J.A. 1976, An investigation of Fitts' law using a wide range of movement amplitudes. *Journal of Motor Behavior* **8**, 113-128.

LASZLO, E. & MASULLI, I. (eds) 1993, *The Evolution of Cognitive Maps* (Gordon & Breach, Amsterdam).

LEWIN, L.M., & WAKEFIELD, J.A. JR. 1979, Percentage agreement and phi: a conversion table. *Journal of Applied Behavior Analysis* **12**, 299-301.

LIEBLICH, I. 1982, Multiple representations of space underlying behavior. *Behavioral & Brain Sciences* **5**, 627-659.

LUNEBERG, G. 1947, *Mathematical Analysis of Binocular Vision* (Princeton University Press, Princeton, NJ).

MACH, E. 1886, *Die Analyse der Empfindungen und das Verhaltnis des Psychischen zun Physischen.* [The Analysis of Sensations and the Relation of the Physical to the Psychical], 5th Ed. (1959)(Dover, New York).

MANDELBROT, B.B. 1975, *Les Objets Fractals: Forme, Hasard et Dimension* (Flammarion, Paris).

MANDELBROT, B.B. 1977, *Fractals: Form, Chance, & Dimension* (W.H. Freeman & Co., San Francisco).

MANDELBROT, B.B. 1982, *The Fractal Geometry of Nature* (W.H. Freeman & Co., New York).

McFARLAND, D. 1985, *Animal Behavior: Psychobiology, Ethology, and Evolution* (Benjamin/Cummings, Menlo Park, CA).

MOORE, G.T. 1975, Spatial relations ability and developmental levels of urban cognitive mapping: a research note. *Man-Environment Systems* **5**, 247-248.

MOOSE, P. 1991, How long is the coastline of a cognitive map? Paper presented to the Inaugural Conference for a Society for Chaos Theory in Psychology, San Francisco, August 15-16.

OLTON, D.S. 1982, Spatially organized behaviors of animals: Behavioral and neurological studies. In M. Potegal (ed), *Spatial Abilities: Development and Physiological Foundations* (Academic Press, New York).

O'NEILL, M. 1991, A biologically based model of spatial cognition and wayfinding. *Journal of Environmental Psychology* **11**, 299-320.

ORNSTEIN, R. 1985, *Psychology: The Study of Human Experience* (Harcourt, Brace, Jovanovich, Orlando, FL).

OTT, D., ECKMILLER, R., & BOCK, O. 1987, A head-mounted device for measurement of pointing to visual targets without seeing the pointing arm. *Vision Research* **27**, 307-309.

PEARCE, P.L. 1977, Mental souvenirs: a study of tourists and their city maps. *Australian Journal of Psychology* **29**, 203-210.

PEITGEN, H.O., JURGENS, H., & SAUPE, D. 1992a, *Fractals for the Classroom, Part One: Introduction to Fractals and Chaos* (Springer-Verlag, New York).

PEITGEN, H.O., JURGENS, H., & SAUPE, D. 1992b, *Fractals for the Classroom, Part Two: Complex systems and Mandelbrot Set* (Springer-Verlag, New York).

PRESSON, C.C., DELANGE, N., & HAZELRIGG, M.D. 1989, Orientation specificity in spatial memory: what makes a path different from a map of the path? *Journal of Experimental Psychology: Learning, Memory, and Cognition* **15**, 887-897.

RIDDOCH, G. 1917, Dissociation of visual perceptions due to occipital injuries, with special reference to appreciation of movement. *Brain* **40**, 15-57.

ROVINE, M.J. & WEISMAN, G.D. 1989, Sketch-map variables as predictors of way-finding performance. *Journal of Environmental Psychology* **9**, 217-232.

SARRAILLE, J.J. & GENTRY, T.A. 1994, The Fractal Factory: a CMC virtual laboratory for instruction & research. In Z. Berge & M. Collins (eds), *Computer mediated communications and the online classroom*, Vol 1, 137-150 (Hampton Press, Cresskill, NJ).

SARRAILLE, J.J. 1991, Developing algorithms for calculating fractal dimensions. Paper presented to the Inaugural Conference for a Society for Chaos Theory in Psychology, San Francisco, August 15-16.

SCHROEDER, M. 1991, *Fractals, Chaos, Power Laws: Minutes From An Infinite Paradise* (W.H. Freeman & Co., New York).

SCHUMACHER, R.M. & GENTNER, D. 1988, Transfer of training as analogical mapping. Special Issue: Human-computer interaction and cognitive engineering. *IEEE Transactions on Systems, Man, & Cybernetics* **18**, 592-600.

SCHMIDT, R., FISCHER, E., HEYDEMANN, M., & HOFFMANN, R. 1991, Searching for interference among consistent and inconsistent editors: the role of analytic and wholistic processing. *Acta Psychologica* **76**, 51-72.

SHEPARD, R.N. 1966, Metric structures in ordinal data. *Journal of Mathematical Psychology* **3**, 287-315.

SHEPARD, R.N. 1974, Representation of structure in similarity data: problems and prospects. *Psychometrika* **39**, 373-421.

SHEPARD, R.N. 1987, Toward a universal law of generalization for psychological science. *Science* **237**, 1317-1323.

SHOLL, M.J. 1987, Cognitive maps as orienting schemata. *Journal of Experimental Psychology: Learning, Memory, and Cognition* **13**, 615-628.

STEEN, L.A. (ed). 1990, *On the Shoulder of Giants: New Approaches to Numeracy* (National Academy Press, Washington).

STUELAND, T. 1993, The Geometry of Imagination II: Using the Fractal Dimension to Search for Relationships between a New Measure of Spatial Cognition and Individual Differences in Personality and Intelligence. Unpublished master's thesis, California State University, Stanislaus, Turlock, CA.

TOLEMAN, E.C. 1948, Cognitive maps in rats and men. *Psychological Review* **55**, 189-208.

WAKEFIELD, J.A. Jr. 1980, Relationship between two expressions of reliability: percentage agreement and phi. *Educational and Psychological Measurement* **40**, 593-597.

WEST, T.G. 1991, *In the Mind's Eye : Visual Thinkers, Gifted People with Learning Difficulties, Computer Images, and the Ironies of Creativity* (Prometheus Books, Buffalo, NY).

WEST, T.G. 1992a, A return to visual thinking: in education and in the workplace, we'll see a higher regard for visualization skills and talents. *Computer Graphics World* **15**, 115.

WEST, T.G. 1992b, A future of reversals: Dyslexic talents in a world of computer visualization. *Annals of Dyslexia* **42**, 124-139.

WEST, T.G. 1993, Visual thinkers in an age of computer visualization: problems and possibilities. Panel presentation at SIGGRAPH Conference, Anaheim, CA, August 3.

WESTHEIMER, G. 1991, Visual discriminations of fractal borders. *Proceedings of the Royal Society of London. Series B: Biological Sciences* **243**, 215-219.

ZHANG, W.R., CHEN, S.S. & BEZDEK, J. C. 1989, Pool2: A generic system for cognitive map development and decision analysis. *IEEE Transactions on Systems, Man, & Cybernetics* **19**, 31-39.

Part 3: Cooperative Work

6

The world view of collaborative tools

MUNIR MANDVIWALLA

Computer and Information Sciences, Temple University, Philadelphia, PA 19122 USA
mandviwa@vm.temple.edu

Abstract. The experiences, biases, and world views of developers of collaborative systems are important factors in understanding the systems' adoption and use. This importance stems from the multiple-user attribute of collaborative tools. When a single-user tool does not match user needs and preferences, the individual user is able to change the tool relatively simply. Users of collaborative tools do not have this luxury, because several people need to use the same system.

This chapter describes relationships among the most common world views employed by developers of collaborative tools, and analyses such world views in terms of their potential to influence users. Adaptive Structuration Theory (Poole & DeSanctis, 1990) is proposed as a way to understand the behaviour and responses of users to the "spirit" or world view of particular tools. This chapter also examines the behavioural feasibility of developing tools to support multiple world views.

1. Introduction

A significant number of collaborative systems have been developed and documented. Researchers refer to these systems with a variety of terms such as Group Decision Support Systems (GDSS), Computer Mediated Communication Systems (CMC), Group Support Systems (GSS), Computer Supported Cooperative Work Systems (CSCW), and Groupware. This paper uses the term "groupware" generically to describe information systems that support collaborative work groups. The experiences, biases, and world views of developers of groupware are important factors in understanding the adoption and use of such tools. Although identifying the world view of developers is an interesting question in itself, several unique attributes of groupware increase the relative importance of the issue.

1.1 *The multi-user component*

Groupware typically has a multiple-user component. When a single-user tool does not match user needs and

preferences, the individual user is able to change the tool relatively simply. Users of collaborative tools do not have this luxury, because several people need to use the same system. For example, one world view in designing a meeting support system is that the leader decides what it is that participants should work on, and when -- even though some participants may strongly prefer the first alternative to the second or vice versa. Another world view is that the leader only selects a general agenda, allowing the flow of a meeting to determine when each agenda item is discussed. A particular system typically only supports one world view.

1.2 *The definition of collaboration*

An examination of world view is important in the area of collaboration support because of fragmented and differing viewpoints on the definition, scope, and goals of collaborative systems. An understanding of world views held by designers who develop GDSS, CSCW, and groupware may bring us closer to a shared, common definition.

1.3 *User-centred design*

The movement toward user-centred design of systems suggests that if world views are in fact attributes of systems, then users should be able to influence or select the systems' world views. An analysis of world views embedded in current approaches should assist users in matching the technology to their needs.

2. What is a world view?

A world view is a belief about how things are or should be. Mechanism, formism, organicism, and contextualism are examples of world views (Pepper, 1942). Whiteside and Wixon (1988) explain that world views offer a coherent and internally consistent view of the world, and note that the analysis of world views is a powerful starting point for examining belief systems. World views influence research. According to Winograd and Flores (1986, p. 24)

> In the day-to-day business of research, writing, and teaching, scientists operate within a background of beliefs about how things are. This background invisibly shapes what they do and how they choose to do it. Systems development research is no exception. All design work involves the explicit or implicit use of design principles that are based on a world view (Winograd, 1986). The principles guide the construction of systems by determining the questions that are raised and the types of solutions that are offered.

3. Origins of groupware world views

World views that influence groupware design originate in the people connected with design of the system. The tool used to develop the system and the environment in which it is developed also may influence the design.

The origin of particular world views may be cultural, experiential, gender-based, organisational, technical, and so on. A world view can vary in scope. Some views reflect our most basic values, such as beliefs about the rights of others. Some reflect specific theories, such as sociotechnical systems theory. Others are aligned with technical views of how a system should operate or be developed, and with skills needed to use the system. For example, developers who have spent most of their professional lives building batch applications may carry over "batch" ideas to interactive applications. Designers, programmers, managers, and users can bring a multitude of world views to a particular systems development project. (A detailed analysis of how a world view is created in different individuals is beyond the scope of this work.)

Subsequent analysis in this chapter assumes the following precepts.

VIEW COMPATIBILITY

A system will reflect a collection of world views that are consistent with each other. This chapter treats the behavioural portions of these views as a whole. The successful completion of a development project may result in a system that exhibits several world views which vary in scope and focus. However, the process of development will result in views that are compatible with each other. Incompatible views will be winnowed out through negotiation and discussion among people involved in the project.

VIEW SOURCE

In current systems, the most important source of the overall world view of a system are its designers and developers, since they have ultimate control over the system.

VIEW FOCUS

This work concentrates on the world views of groupware design work in research institutions, as reflected in published papers written by the designers and developers themselves.

VIEW INDEPENDENCE

This chapter also assumes that artefacts can represent world views independent of an observer. Later discussion describes how an observer can discover and appropriate a new perceived world view.

4. World view and adaptive structuration

Poole and DeSanctis (1990) propose "adaptive structuration" theory as a tool for understanding the adoption of GDSS. The components of their theory include:

SYSTEM
A social entity (e.g., a group that demonstrates an observable pattern of relations).

STRUCTURES
The rules and resources used by actors to generate and sustain the system. Structures are drawn from social institutions or are provided through technology.

SPIRIT
An aspect of technological structure. The spirit comprises the goals and attitudes that the technology promotes.

STRUCTURAL FEATURES
Another aspect of technological structure. Structural features are the specific rules and resources built into the technology.

STRUCTURATION
The process that describes the group's creation and use of structures.

APPROPRIATION
Each group forms its own particular collection of structural features. The collection of features is appropriated from social institutions and technology. Appropriations

can be faithful to the spirit of the technology, or ironic.

According to Poole and DeSanctis (p. 180)

> When a group uses a voting procedure built into a GDSS, it is employing these rules to act, but -- more than this -- it is reminding itself that these rules exist, working out a way of using the rules, perhaps creating a special version of them; in short, it is producing and re-producing the rules for its present and future use.

Adaptive Structuration Theory (AST) is well-suited for analysing the influence of world views embedded in systems by designers, because it explicitly differentiates "spirit" from "structural features". Other theories usually treat the system as a black box or as a collection of features. In the context of this chapter, the "spirit" of a system is analogous to the world view of the system. Structural features are the specific technological design strategies that implement the spirit.

5. World views

Researchers have discussed the world views of collaborative research in general, and of collaborative systems in particular. For example, Steiner (1986) traces the underlying views affecting social psychological research on groups. Grudin (1991) contrasts views aligned with the internal development of collaborative systems with views aligned with packaged software. Galegher & Kraut (1990) contrast prescriptive and permissive designs. DeSanctis (1993) contrasts individualism and democratic views with collectivism.

Since the purpose of this chapter is to analyse world views in terms of their potential to influence users, we need to examine directly the views that are being used to develop systems.

An organisational scheme for direct analysis of world views is developed next.

The scheme follows a substrate structure (see Figure 1). At the first level, the "basic technological world views" describe perceptions about the role and purpose of technology. These perceptions influence the views that follow. The second level contains specific views. These views are grouped together under "Developmental", "Invention of artefacts", and "Collaboration map" labels. Specific views are described in terms of their behavioural beliefs about the appropriate characteristics of computer support for collaboration. Such beliefs influence the spirit and structural features of a system.

At the final level is "design strategy", which reflects beliefs about the ways of developing computer support for collaboration. These beliefs influence structural features incorporated into the system. The behavioural world view (spirit) and design strategy (structural features) are sepa-

rated in my analysis because they do not experience a one-to-one correspondence. In other words, a behavioural world view may lead to more than one design strategy.

BASIC TECHNOLOGICAL WORLD VIEWS
Technological determinism
Technological emergence
Interactive determinism
Socio-technical approach
--
SPECIFIC GROUPWARE WORLD VIEWS
Developmental
Invention of artefacts
Collaboration map
--
DESIGN STRATEGY
(various)

Figure 1. An organizational scheme for analysis of world views

This chapter uses the term "world view" for all these levels, although the term may in fact be ill-suited to the lower levels. This usage is consistent with the meaning of world view taken in this chapter: *a belief about how things are or should be*. The organisational scheme in Figure 1 is motivated by a desire to examine the user effects of views embedded in system designs. Therefore, the scheme evolves from general beliefs to specific design strategies. There are, however, other potential classification schemes (see Whiteside & Wixon, 1988).

The basic technological world views in Figure 1 are based on Majchrzak and Davis (1990); specific groupware world views (and design strategy) are based on the author's subjective interpretation. An objective and replicatable method of identifying views would have been preferable. This is a problem, because any analysis of world view is necessarily coloured by the observer's own world view. Nevertheless, in this analysis every effort was made to ensure that identified world views are consistent with their original vision. This was accomplished through careful examination of multiple papers written by people involved in development of groupware, and by direct examination of some systems.

From the perspective of this chapter, the world view of a system may be different from the world view of researchers experimenting with the system, which itself may be different from the world view of those who built the system. The system world view also may be different from the user world view created when users interact with the system. Of most interest is the world view embedded in the system design.

6. Technological world views

World views at this level come from beliefs about the role and application of technology. Analysis at this level is based on work done by Majchrzak and Davis in computer integrated manufacturing (CIM). Although factory automation may seem at first glance to be quite different from collaboration, there are some similarities. According to Majchrzak and Davis (1990), workers in CIM factories must be adept at solving abstract problems and in performing unstructured tasks. Production frequently requires team effort; decision making authority must be distributed further down the line, therefore mutual dependencies are created. This also is true of team based office work. Majchrzak and Davis identify four "approaches" (world views) that have been used to study human issues relating to technology implementation. This chapter suggests that these world views also can be used to understand the design of groupware.

6.1 *Technological determinism*

Determinism is the view that the introduction of new technology has predictable consequences. The assumption is that the relationship between technology and human behaviour is unidirectional (Spacapan & Oskamp, 1990). Technological determinism "views technology as an exogenous force which determines or strongly constrains the behaviour of individuals and organisations" (Markus & Robey, 1988, p. 585, cited in Majchrzak & Davis, 1990).

With respect to groupware, the deterministic developer assumes that the introduction of technology can alter group behaviour significantly. For example, designs for COORDINATOR (Da Vinci Systems, 1991) and for GROUPSYSTEMS (Ventana, 1992) may be labelled deterministic. The deterministic view encourages the developer to explore design choices that can alter group behaviour.

Some researchers have labelled one version of this view "utopianism", the placement of a specific technology as the central enabler of an utopian vision (Dunlop & Kling, 1991). In the groupware context, utopianism would appear as a belief that technology can solve all collaboration problems. For example, there is an assumption in COORDINATOR that many communication problems would be solved if people were to follow the Speech Act Taxonomy. Utopianism also assumes that technology can achieve a set of utopian goals regardless of human behaviour. For example, the interface design for COORDINATOR makes it difficult for people to avoid the Speech Act Taxonomy in their electronic communication. And in GROUPSYSTEMS, the interface is designed so that participants can work only on the topic selected by the facilitator.

Another version of the utopian view has been labelled "egalitarian": the act of focusing only on the positive aspects of collaboration while ignoring status, power, and interest differences among group members (Kling, 1991). For example, Grudin (1988) found that group calendaring was problematic because the software assumed that everybody in the organisation had the resources and inclination to share their (what used to be private) calendars with everybody else.

6.2 *Technological emergence*

Emergence is the view that the introduction of new technology causes a "dynamic interplay among workers, managers, technology, and organisational context" (Majchrzak and Davis, 1990, p. 42). This interplay of complex social interaction among people, roles, and objectives enabled by new technology is said to result in organisational change. Researchers applying an emergent world view may experience results similar to those of Bullen and Bennett (1990). They found that COORDINATOR users ignored features that organise different types of "speech acts" into linked "conversations". Instead, they used the software as an electronic mail package. In other words, although the world view of COORDINATOR may have been deterministic, users appropriated the software to fit a less deterministic world view. Bullen and Bennett were able to identify this user action as being of interest because the researchers were themselves following an emergent world view.

With respect to groupware design, the developer may assume that new technology is but one of many determinants of organisational change. Since the developer cannot predict social dynamics, he or she may decide to concentrate on refining and inventing new technological artefacts that have more to do with technical goals than with social understanding. The developer (or another researcher) then might gather usage data on the new tool and attempt to explain results using an interconnected web of factors. Results often are inconclusive, since the tool design was not based on a theory of user behaviour.

Many early groupware packages adopted the emergence world view by default. Their developers were faced with only general frameworks of workgroup behaviour (Goodman, Ravlin & Schminke, 1990) and with contingent variables such as task and environment, and composition (Gladstein, 1984). Their situation was compounded by significant technical challenges. It is not surprising that many early groupware developers concentrated on inventing new collaborative artefacts.

6.3 *Interactive determinism*

A hybrid of the first two views, interactive determinism assumes that some aspects of organisational change are brought about directly as a result of new technology, while other aspects emerge from social interaction. This view holds that social aspects cannot be predicted from knowledge of technology alone. This view is the meeting point of the "results oriented" emergent developer and the "socially aware" deterministic developer. Most current groupware follows this view, regardless of whether the original view was emergent or deterministic.

One way to characterise early groupware development is to suggest that research in GDSS followed a deterministic world view, while early research in CSCW followed an emergent world view. However, this generalisation does not apply fully, given the wide variety of approaches used by developers in both areas.

6.4 *Socio-technical approach*

The socio-technical approach is based on the view that organisations must optimise the functioning of both technical and social systems (Majchrzak & Davis, 1990; Bostrom & Heinen, 1977). The "technical system" refers to components that contribute to the task accomplishment goals of the organisation; the "social system" refers to quality of work life goals. According to Majchrzak and Davis (1990), the socio-technical approach is different from others in that it does not view technology as a fixed phenomenon (the emergent and interactive approaches view technology as a given, whose usage can be adapted for different needs).

In the groupware context, a socio-technical approach implies a study of user requirements, an understanding of various technical options, and a conscious attempt to match technology to requirements. This approach is commonplace and taken for granted by "systems analysts." However, achieving it has been difficult in groupware development because early researchers were faced with very little knowledge of collaborative work and of technical options.

6.5 *Adaptive structuration*

It is interesting to observe that Adaptive Structuration Theory works with all of these views. For example, a developer following a deterministic approach can be concerned with ensuring faithful appropriation of structural features, while the emergent developer can use AST as a way to test social implications of design.

However, in full use AST lends itself to the socio-technical approach. For example, a developer may design structural features in such a way that they can be appropriated easily by the group. Then, specific world views may be examined in the context of the technological world view. Next, the terminology of adaptive structura-

tion is used to describe the design's spirit and structural features.

7. Groupware world views

7.1 *Developmental*

Those holding this view are interested in repairing and enhancing the processes of collaboration and meeting (hence the label "developmental"). The developmental world view is rooted in studies of group development that have pinpointed dysfunctional group behaviours (e.g., scapegoating and unequal participation; see McCollom, 1990, for an overview). These group behaviours also are known as process losses (Steiner, 1972).

The developmental world view seeks to minimise process losses and to increase process gains, in the context of decision making-oriented collaborative activity. These objectives are achieved typically via structures applied to group interaction through the software and by a human facilitator. The best examples can be found in DeSanctis and Gallupe (1987) and in Nunamaker et al (1991). Commercial and prototype systems developed with this view (e.g., GROUPSYSTEMS) have a deterministic flavour. However, most empirical research studying these systems follows what Majchrzak and Davis call "interactive determinism".

The developmental world view is implemented in systems using a combination of the following design strategies.

ACTIVITY DRIVEN

Huber (1984) concludes that it may not be possible to design a generalised GDSS, because the possible decision-group tasks are beyond enumeration. Huber suggests an activity driven (as opposed to task driven) design strategy. This strategy is based on the view that no matter what tasks a group may engage in, its members will be carrying out one or more of the following activities: information retrieval (or generation), information sharing, information use. Applications of this strategy develop structural features in the system based on this activity typology.

INFORMATION EXCHANGE

According to DeSanctis and Gallupe (1987), decision making occurs through interpersonal communication, which in turn is based on the exchange of information among group members. Changing the pattern of interpersonal communication in a positive direction is one way to support group decision making through technology. Applications of this strategy develop structural features that can change the patterns of interaction within a group.

SHELL

According to DeSanctis and Gallupe (1987), it is not possible to create an architecture suitable for all group decision support situations. There is considerable variation in information exchange patterns across groups; no one generalised decision making style is effective for all groups. Therefore, the authors recommend a structural feature called a "shell" that supports the generation of different tools.

7.2 *Invention of artefacts*

Those holding this view focus on development of novel collaboration structural features (artefacts), such as shared environments and drawing tools. Because research in this category does not necessarily start with a well-articulated behavioural spirit, it is difficult to label the work generically. A behavioural world view sometimes is generated following a bottom-up approach in which the researcher first develops the artefact, then develops explanations for how the artefact will influence behaviour. This may be done by connecting the artefact with current theories or by developing new behavioural models. Studies of systems that are developed in this "invention" mode usually follow an emergent or interactive determinism approach. Examples of such design strategies include:

SHARED WORKSPACE

This strategy is based on abstracting the concept of a chalkboard to WYSIWIS (what you see is what I see) views of workstations (Stefik et al, 1987). Workstations in a meeting room are synchronised so they provide a shared, focused workspace for group work. Tools are implemented to support tasks in this shared workspace. More recent versions of this strategy have loosened the synchronisation among stations, but kept the concept of a shared common workspace. The most important structural feature in this strategy is the shared workspace.

CONTINUITY WITH DESKTOP

This strategy extends the shared workspace to incorporate two existing individual workspaces: computers and physical desktops (Ishi, 1990). This extension is accomplished with a virtual shared workspace in which users can interact, by sharing their computer screen (for concurrent pointing, writing, drawing), by sharing their physical desktop, and by using a live audio-visual communications link, for face-to-face conversation.

7.3 *The collaboration map*

The collaboration map groups views that range from deterministic to socio-technical. Here, the researcher is interested in modeling collaborative behaviour and in implementing systems based on such models. Alternatively, the researcher may focus on a particular sub-domain of collaboration (such as collaborative authoring), deriving behavioural views to mirror domain-specific issues.

Continuing with the map metaphor, world views described below can be differentiated by the topographical features they emphasise. The "language action" view focuses on the semantics of speech used for interaction among group members; the "life world" view targets daily mundane activities that surround office work and interaction; "coordination theory" centres on interdependent activities and processes that make up coordinated work. Although the language action view does not have a technological world view per se, implementations of this view have had a deterministic flavour. The lifeworld view is emergent, while studies of coordination seem closest to the socio-technical approach because of their focus on customisation.

LANGUAGE ACTION

The language action view holds that the lifeblood of an organisation is neither data nor computation, but interaction (Winograd & Flores, 1986; Winograd, 1986). Work in an organisation consists of a network of interlinked interactions or actions. The language applied and the meaning embedded in the use of words serve as starting points for establishing a network of interconnected actions. Language comprises syntax (the rules of structure), semantics (the relationship between structures and meanings), and pragmatics (action and context).

The action component of pragmatics originates from Speech Act Theory. Speech acts capture the actions or suggestions for action embedded in sentences. The focus of the language action view is to start at the structure of work embodied in the actions and context surrounding pragmatics, then to use that structure to study the forms of interaction. This view has guided the design of systems such as COSMOS (Bowers & Churcher, 1988), COORDINATOR (Da Vinci Systems, 1991), and MEETING MEMORY (Sandoe et al, 1991).

The most common structural features used to implement the language action world view are speech acts, applied to structure communication -- for example, the addition of speech act-based templates to an electronic mail system.

LIFEWORLD AND WORKADAY WORLD

"Lifeworld" is a term is used to describe the daily world (Schutz & Luckman, 1973). According to Moran & Anderson (1990), the lifeworld is the mundane everyday activities, relationships, knowledge, and technological and other resources that comprise the day-to-day world we take for granted, are largely unaware of, and usually do not question. The Workaday World view holds that technology is part of the lifeworld and can be understood from the perspective of people working in the lifeworld (Moran & Anderson 1990). Those holding this view examine the relationship between working life and technology. Interrelated components of the Workaday World are technologies, sociality, and work practice. Examples of this view can be found in research at Xerox EuroParc on multimedia environments (see Moran & Anderson, 1990).

The design strategy for implementing this view focuses on multimedia technologies. The modality and richness of the technologies media provide structural features of the view. The several media provide ways to support and extend the range of possible social encounters in a work day.

COORDINATION THEORY

Malone and Crowston (1990) suggest another view, "Coordination Theory" -- the interdisciplinary study of coordination that can be used in the design of cooperative tools. Coordination is the act of working together harmoniously (including both cooperation and conflict). The narrow definition of coordination is the act of managing interdependencies between activities performed to achieve a goal. Interdependence is important because if there is no interdependence, there is nothing to coordinate.

Interdependence between activities can be analysed in terms of common objects involved in both activities (objects that constrain activities). Different patterns of use for common objects will result in different kinds of interdependencies. The types of interdependence recognised by Malone and Crowston are prerequisite, shared resource, and simultaneity (the time at which more than one activity must occur).

A situation may be characterised in terms of the interdependencies that it involves. The coordination process can be described by successively deeper levels of underlying process. The initial level is coordination (goals, activities, actors, resources, and interdependencies), then group decision making (goals, actors, alternatives, evaluations, and choices), then communications (senders, receivers, messages, and languages), and lastly perception of common objects (actors and objects). Examples of this view can be found in Lai and Malone (1988), which describes development of the OBJECT LENS system.

The Coordination Theory strategy is based on providing users with the structural features to create their own cooperative applications (Lai & Malone, 1988). These structured building blocks are semi-structured objects and

agents. Semi-structured objects are used to define information templates; agents are used to define rules that act upon information in the objects.

8. The effects of world view

The effects of world view can be analysed in terms of situations in which the view will be important to users. These situations include matching the system to the user, training, the impact on users, and customisation.

8.1 *Matching system to user*

Knowledge of the world view implemented in groupware can help a group decide whether to adopt the system. For example, software developers could describe the spirit of the system in their product literature. Users then could decide whether the spirit of the system and the system's corresponding structural features match their needs. The process of fitting world view to user is important, because world view-related constraints will influence the overall appearance and operation of a system. Matching these constraints to the needs of users is particularly important for collaborative applications. If the world view of a system does not match all of the (potentially different) users, then some users may decide to stop using the system. This is problematic, because a collaborative application needs multiple users if it's going to be successful (Grudin, 1988).

Fitting the world view to the user also is attractive because a particular world view may be demonstrably superior or more desirable in a given context. A group that is undergoing social and morale problems may be better served by a system that supports a developmental view. For example, GROUPSYSTEMS (Ventana, 1992) -- with its emphasis on consensus building and information sharing -- may help a group overcome problems of communication and trust. A long lived group whose members are comfortable with each other and whose objectives are clear-cut may be better served by a system that provides simple collaborative artefacts, rather than one that tries to develop the artefacts or to impose a model of collaboration (such as a shared whiteboard system for occasional brainstorming)

Further research is needed to map characteristics of groups to potential world views. However, there are practical difficulties in fitting world views to users. Although researchers are necessarily concerned with world view, a commercial developer may have no interest in this issue. A group that is presented with the world view of a system may not know what to do with such information. That is, the group may be unable to translate abstract descriptions into the specifics of its situation. A group also may be unaware of its own world view or of its world view preferences.

8.2 *Training*

Poole and DeSanctis (1990) hypothesise that if users have knowledge of the spirit of their system, then it is more likely that their appropriation will be faithful. Training materials for a system can focus on helping the user learn both the structural features of the system and its spirit. Knowledge of the spirit also may help new users predict the syntax of commands and the presence of structural features. Such knowledge may help users realise the potential domains of application for the system.

8.3 *Impact on users*

According to Adaptive Structuration Theory, the process of structuration results in a group appropriating structural features of a system for the group's own use. Their appropriation may be faithful or ironic to the spirit of the system and to its structural features.

The world view's impact on users can be analysed at several levels. At a macro level, the influence of system-based world view can be positive, if the view enables the group to accomplish its objectives. The accomplishment of objectives can be further sub-divided into task accomplishment and attainment of social goals. For example, the world view of a system may structure group interaction in such a way that dysfunctional behaviour among members is reduced (or the structure may force a group to address dysfunctions directly). Such a structuring may allow a group to complete its task successfully, in minimum time.

On the other hand, the effect of a system-based world view may be negative, if it frustrates goals or if it creates social problems (such as low morale). Clearly, it is possible for a view to have a positive influence in one dimension, but a negative influence in another.

At a more detailed level of analysis, it is useful to consider the differential effects of world view on the individuals that comprise and supervise a group. For example, the world view of a system may be interpreted differently by a manager supervising the performance of a group, by a leader responsible for the actions taken by a group, and by individual group members. One set of individuals may perceive a system-based world view in a positive manner, while others see it as negative.

According to Poole and DeSanctis (1990), the actions of a leader may influence how well other members perceive the world view of a system. Moreover, some world views influence the role of the leader. For example, a developmental world view may increase the role and responsibilities of a leader, while an artefact world view may assign no specific role to the leader. GROUPSYSTEMS, for example, increases the importance of the group leader or facilitator.

Thus far, the analysis has assumed that world view is static. According to Adaptive Structuration Theory, a group can adapt the world view and its structural features to the group's needs. Further, the respective constituencies may react differently to different adaptations. For example, a manager may be displeased at an ironic appropriation (but later pleased when the appropriation results in successful task accomplishment).

A process of negotiation may take place among the various constituencies in a group as it slowly appropriates the system. This negotiation may not focus explicitly on adapting the world view, but instead may be part of other social processes. For example, an influential group member may convince the leader to adjust the system to correspond to the member's mental model and way of working. It may be possible to interpret interaction among group members as the negotiation of world views appropriation.

8.4 *Customisation*

The analysis thus far also has assumed that the world view of a system and the system's structural features are malleable in ways important to perceptions and use. Another way to examine these issues is in terms of tool customisation. Most modern systems offer extensive customisation options, ranging from low level individual options (e.g., set colour) to larger group level options (e.g., select among different tools or set menu appearance (Mandviwalla, 1994).

Group level customisation may allow a group to adjust the world view of the technology. (However, complete customisability may never be possible, due to technical constraints.) In the context of adaptive structuration, this means that group members may be able to modify the spirit and structural features of the system. For example, the OBJECT LENS system described by Lai and Malone (1988) and the CGS ENVIRONMENT system described by Mandviwalla et al (1991) include group level customisation options.

Selectable world views would facilitate customisation. Although some researchers have advocated paradigmatic pluralism at the conceptual level (Moran & Anderson, 1990), most existing systems do not support more than one world view. Instead, the user must appropriate features in order to customise the system. A selectable world view might be implemented by allowing users to select from sets of customisation options, analogous to the "style" sheets available in modern world processors.

The use of customable systems considerably increases the range of options for negotiation among the leader (and/or system administrator) and group members. Adapting the world view of a system and its structural features to the needs of the group falls within the socio-technical approach. It may be useful to interpret negotiation among group members about customisation options as a process of jointly optimising the technology and the social goals of the group.

Before considering this negotiation process, it is important to ask whether such negotiation will in fact occur -- and if it does occur, whether the process is likely to have a beneficial result. Will the users of collaborative software, faced with the inherent complexities of routine use, even consider using customisation options?

It is possible that users may stop using a system if "default" options do not satisfy their needs or match their individual world views. It also is possible that forcing users to select one of a number of world views prior to system usage may surface conflicts that ordinarily would not appear in a one world view system. As discussed previously, users may not be able to understand such abstract descriptions of world views and may not be able to align the descriptions with their needs and desires. Moreover, the process of thinking about these issues may lead users to compare their mental models to the mental models of other members in the group. Negotiation could degenerate into a stand-off, with nobody willing to abandon their preferred mental model. By contrast, a one world view system would present the group with an immutable given, an environment that although inflexible would not distract them from their task accomplishment goals.

Further insight could be gained in empirical studies that manipulate world view and record effects of those manipulations. Such studies will need to operationalise important structural features of the system. Silver (1991) proposes that two important structural features of decision support systems are restrictiveness and guidance. Mandviwalla (1994) expands these human-to-computer characteristics to include structures that describe human-to-human interaction in groupware, including the level of synchronisation among group members and the type of work support (group versus individual). Day (1993) proposes a three dimensional typology of constraints that can be used to measure the effect of these structural features.

9. Summary

The world view of groupware will influence its adoption and use. This chapter identifies world views used by systems development researchers. The views are presented as part of a structure that can be used to understand the relationships within and effects of each view. Adaptive Structuration Theory is used to describe world views, and to analyse the effects of world views on users.

References

BOSTROM, R. P. & HEINEN, S. 1977,. MIS problems and failures: a socio-technical perspective, Part I. *MIS Quarterly* **1** (3) (September), 17-32.

BOWERS, J., & CHURCHER, J. 1988, Local and global structuring of computer mediated communication: developing linguistic perspectives on CSCW in COSMOS. *CSCW Proceedings 1988*, 125-139.

BULLEN, C. & BENNETT, J. 1991, Groupware in practice: an interpretation of work experiences. In Dunlop, C. & Kling, R. (eds), *Computerization & Controversy*, 257-287 (Academic Press, Boston).

DA VINCI SYSTEMS 1991, Coordinator II [software]. (Da Vinci Systems Corporation, Raleigh, NC).

DAY, D.L. 1993, Precis of behavioral and perceptual responses to constraint management in computer-mediated design activities", *Electronic Journal of Communication* [On-Line] **3** (2). Guest editor: Thomas Benson. Available e-mail: Comserve@Vm.its.rpi.edu. Message: Send Day V3N293.

DESANCTIS, G. & GALLUPE, R. B. 1987, A foundation for the study of group decision support systems. *Management Science*, **33** (5), 589-609.

DESANCTIS, G. 1993, Shifting foundations in group support systems research. In Jessup, L. & Valacich, J. (eds), *Group Support Systems: New Perspectives*, 97-111 (Macmillan, New York).

DUNLOP, C. & KLING, R. 1991, The dreams of technological utopianism. In Dunlop, C. & Kling, R. (eds), *Computerization & Controversy*, 14-29 (Academic Press,. Boston).

FLORES, F., GRAVES, M., HARTFIELD, B., & WINOGRAD, T. 1988, Computer systems and the design of organizational interaction. *ACM Transactions on Office Information Systems*, **6** (2), 153-172.

GALEGHER, J. & KRAUT, R. 1990, Technology for intellectual teamwork: perspectives on research and design. In Galegher, J., Kraut, R., & Egido, C. (eds), *Intellectual Teamwork*, 1-20 (Lawrence Erlbaum Associates, Hillsdale, NJ).

GLADSTEIN, D. 1984, Groups in context: a model of task group effectiveness. *Administrative Science Quarterly* **29**, 499-517.

GOODMAN, P., RAVLIN, E., & SCHMINKE, M. 1990, Understanding groups in organizations. In Cummings, L. L. & Shaw, B. (eds), *Leadership, Participation, and Group Behavior*, 333-385 (JAI Press, London).

GRUDIN, J. 1991, CSCW: The convergence of two development contexts. *CHI Proceedings 1991*, 91-97 (ACM, New York).

GRUDIN, J. 1988, Why CSCW applications fail: problems

in the design and evaluation of organizational interfaces. *CSCW Proceedings 1988*, 85-93 (ACM, New York).

GUTEK, B. 1990, Work group structure and information technology: a structural contingency approach. In Galegher, J., Kraut, R., & Egido, C. (eds), *Intellectual Teamwork*, 63-78 (Lawrence Erlbaum Associates, Hillsdale, NJ).

HUBER, G. P. 1989, Issues in the design of group decision support systems. *MIS Quarterly* 3, 195-204.

ISHII, H. 1990, TeamWorkStation: towards a seamless shared workspace. *CSCW Proceedings* 1990, 13-26 (ACM, New York).

KLING, R. 1991, Cooperation, coordination, and control in computer supported cooperative work. *Communications of the ACM* **34** (12), 83-88.

LAI, K. & MALONE, T. 1988, Object lens: a "spreadsheet" for cooperative work. *CSCW Proceedings 1988*, 115-124 (ACM, New York).

MAJCHRZAK, A. & DAVIS, D. 1990, The human side of flexible factory automation: research and management practice. In Oskamp, S. & Spacapan, S. (eds), *Peoples Reaction to Technology: The Claremont Symposium on Applied Social Psychology*, 33-65. (Sage Publications, Newbury Park, CA).

MALONE, T. & CROWSTON, K. 1990, What is coordination theory and how can it help design cooperative work systems? *CSCW Proceedings 1990*, 357-370 (ACM, New York).

MANDVIWALLA, M. 1994, The Design of Group Support Systems: Generic Requirements, Design Framework, Systems Development Strategies, and a Case Study. Unpublished Ph.D. dissertation, Claremont Graduate School Programs in Information Science (January).

MANDVIWALLA, M., GRAY, P., OLFMAN, L., & SATZINGER, J. 1991, The CGS environment. *HICSS Proceedings*, Vol. III, 600-607 (Hawaii International Conference on System Sciences).

MARKUS, M. L. & ROBEY, D. 1988, Information technology and organizational change: causal structure in theory and research. *Management Science* **34**, 583-597.

MCCOLLOM, M. 1990, Reevaluating group development: a critique of familiar models. In Gillette, J. & McCollom, M. (eds), *Groups in Context*, 133-154 (Addison-Wesley, Reading, MA).

MORAN, T. P. & ANDERSON, R. J. 1990, The workaday world as a paradigm for CSCW design. *CSCW Proceedings 1990*, 381-393 (ACM, New York).

NUNAMAKER, J. F., DENNIS, A., VALACICH, J. S., VOGEL, D. R., & GEORGE, J. 1991, Electronic meeting systems to support group work. *Communications of the ACM* **34** (7), 40-61.

PEPPER, S. 1988, *World Hypotheses*, 1942 (University of California Press, Berkeley, CA). Referenced in Whiteside and Wixon, 1988.

POOLE, M. & DESANCTIS, G. 1990, Understanding the use of group decision support systems: the theory of adap-

tive structuration. In Fulk, J. & Steinfield, C. (eds), *Organizations and Communication Technology*, 173-193 (Sage Publications, Newbury Park, CA).

SANDOE, K., OLFMAN, L., & MANDVIWALLA, M. 1991, Meeting in time: recording the work group conversation. *ICIS Proceedings 1991*, 261-271 (International Conference on Information Systems).

SCHUTZ, A. & LUCKMAN, T. 1973, *The Structures of the Life-World* (Northwestern University Press, Evanston, IL).

SILVER, M. 1991, *Systems that Support Decision Makers* (John Wiley & Sons, Chichester, UK).

SPACAPAN, S. & OSKAMP, S. 1990, Peoples reaction to technology. In Oskamp, S. & Spacapan, S. (eds), *Peoples Reaction to Technology: The Claremont Symposium on Applied Social Psychology*, 9-29. (Sage Publications, Newbury Park, CA).

STEFIK, M., FOSTER, G., BOBROW, D., KAHN, K., LANNING, S., AND SUCHMAN, L. 1987, Beyond the chalkboard: computer support for collaboration and problem solving in meetings. *Communications of the ACM* **30** (1), 32-47.

STEINER, I. 1972, *Group Process and Productivity* (Academic Press, New York).

STEINER, I. 1986, Paradigms and groups. *Advances in Experimental Social Psychology* **19**, 251-289.

VENTANA 1992, GroupSystems [software] (Ventana Corporation, Tucson, AZ).

WHITESIDE, J. & WIXON, D. 1988, Contextualism as a world view for the reformation of meetings. *CSCW Proceedings 1988*, 369-376 (ACM, New York).

WINOGRAD, T. 1986, A language/action perspective on the design of cooperative work. *CSCW Proceedings 1986*, 203-220 (ACM, New York).

WINOGRAD, T. & FLORES, F. 1986, *Understanding Computers and Cognition* (Ablex, Norwood, NJ).

7

Computer-based simulation models for problem-solving: communicating problem understandings

RAY PAUL* AND PETER THOMAS**

* Dept. of Computer Science and Information Systems, Brunel University, Uxbridge, Middlesex UB8 3PH, UK
   Ray.Paul@brunel.ac.uk
** Centre for Personal Information Management, University of the West of England-Bristol, Coldharbour Lane, Bristol BS16 1QY, UK
   Peter.Thomas@pat.uwe.ac.uk

Abstract. A recognition that computer-based tools communicate mental models among developers, users and other stakeholders, thereby placing constraints on the use of those tools, is important to understanding the use of technology. In our work in computer-based simulation modelling, the realisation that technology can both impose constraints and provide possibilities has been a constant concern.

Computer-based simulation models aid the process of formulating a problem. Such models can act as "dynamic intermediaries" which facilitate the ebb and flow of understanding among stakeholders. This facilitation effect leads to a particular view of the role of technology in decision support. It has enabled us to develop software which improves the process of communicating problem understandings. This chapter describes the use and theoretical foundations of computer-based tools we have developed to support simulation modelling.

1. Introduction

The concept of "mental model" has acquired currency in research literature about the design of computer systems. In fact, the notion of a mental model as a "psychological working model of a system" (Johnson-Laird, 1983) is one of the cornerstones of human-computer interaction (HCI) research and of user interface design. (See Carroll and Olsen, 1988; Briggs, 1988; Carroll and Rosson, 1987; Fischer, 1991; Lewis, 1986; Norman, 1987 and 1983; Gentner and Stevens, 1983.)

Studies have described possible types of (DuBoulay, 1981), strategies for eliciting mental models from users (Halasz and Moran, 1983; Young, 1981), how such models can be tailored and adapted (Carroll and Carrithers, 1984), and the reasoning strategies on which models are based (Riley, 1986).

In user interface design, the notion of mental models has been of practical use. Norman's (1983) distinctions among "design model", "user model", and "system image" have enabled interface designers to draw systematically on users' mental models (Bewlay et al, 1983). By paying careful attention to the conceptual model presented to the user (including manuals, training, and documentation as part of the system image), a user interface can selectively encourage the development of more accurate and more complete user models of the system.

1.1 *Problems with "mental models"*

Several points about this formulation of "mental models" are worth noting.

First, even though the power of constraints imposed by a design model has been recognised, there has been little study of the way in which the HCI design process can be manipulated systematically to good effect -- despite voluminous research. (See Bellotti, 1988 and 1990; Curtis et al, 1988; Dagwell and Weber, 1983; Gould and Lewis, 1985; Gould et al, 1987; Hammond et al, 1983; Farooq and Dominick, 1988; Johnson and Nicolosi, 1990.)

For example, recent approaches such as "Design Rationale" (MacLean et al, 1990) tend to focus on structuring the process of design. Studies which aim to illuminate the designer-user relationship only address the ways in which users' "situated understandings" are structured (Suchman, 1987).

Second, the notion of "mental model" is defined typically in individualistic terms. In this view, mental models are employed by individuals (designers or users) as a way of understanding actions, events and objects. This definition contradicts a growing understanding that users' understandings of systems and their use is "socially constructed". (See Heath and Luff 1991; Winograd 1987; Lawrence et al, 1995; Randall and Hughes, 1995.)

For example, accounts of the implementation failures of large-scale systems (Paul, 1993) have demonstrated that the influence of users, designers and stakeholders -- and the constraints under which systems are developed -- are far more influential than the individual user's understanding of a system.

Third, the usual definition of "mental model" is predominantly mechanistic. This is to be expected, due to HCI's foundation in information processing models of cognition (Card et al, 1983) -- despite arguments which suggest that creating sufficiently powerful, generalisable and useful theories on this basis is problematic (Landauer, 1983).

Fourth, one of the defining features of much work in HCI -- that human-computer interaction is a matter of "interacting" with computers (Nickerson, 1976) -- has suggested that a user's mental model is built in response to the actions of an interactive partner (Luff et al, 1991; Norman and Thomas, 1991). This approach runs counter to suggestions that human-computer interaction is fundamentally a "media process" (Bodker 1991).

Finally, despite the growing body of work in disciplines such as Computer-Supported Cooperative Work (CSCW), system and application design still focuses predominantly on the individual user of a single system. The broader contexts in which users work is regarded largely as of secondary importance.

However, the fact that there are many stakeholders clearly is important in many technologies. In the case of computer-based simulation modeling, many applications are large-scale commercial ventures in which the various agenda of stakeholders embody competing views of how to employ expensive resources. Tension exists between those competing agenda and the need to arrive at a solution which will satisfy all stakeholders' interests to an acceptable extent.

For example, El Sheikh et al (1987) report on the use of a simulation model in planning future berth requirements for a Third World shipping port. Stakeholders consisted of the port authority, the government, an international funding agency, a company of consulting engineers, and an operations research specialist. The port authority required that the new port be adequate to handle their estimate of berth requirements; the government -- anxious to secure funding -- required that the development be as large as possible; the World Bank, who were to fund the development, were concerned that expenditures on construction work be minimised; the consulting engineers were anxious to secure a contract for development of the port.

This example demonstrates the power of computer-based simulation for handling a potentially difficult situation. Although the results of the simulation were reasonably well known, the model's benefits derived from the discussion that took place *around* the results: Participants suggested that their viewpoints might be different if parameters changes were made. The simulation model made rapid testing of such parameter changes possible, with the result that some if not all of the suggestions made were in fact infeasible.

1.2 *Enriching the concept of "mental model"*

As a consequence of these observations, it seems to us that a richer formulation of "mental model" should encompass the ways in which computer technology is embedded in complex contexts, stakeholder (designer and user) activities, and tasks.

A corollary to this need for reformulation is appreciation that technology is partly a "communication medium for understandings". For example, the development of applications such as CASE tools involves a mapping of tool designers' mental models of design processes onto the behaviour of tool users. Similarly, the development of "productivity applications" such as word processors, diarisers and personal information managers (Thomas, 1995) involves the mapping of designers' understandings of those tasks onto the ways in which such tasks are to be performed by users. Of course, from one perspective the issue is trivial, in that all design -- from art, through architecture, to the design of everyday artefacts -- involves some sort of mapping between design intent and eventual use. What is more interesting is how to direct and exploit the relationships among designers, artefacts and users so that systems are made more usable.

In our work on computer-based simulation modelling, a recognition of the ways in which technology can both impose constraints and provide possibilities has been a constant concern. The contribution that computer-based simulation models can make (aiding the process of formulating complex problems) rests on the assumption that such models act as "dynamic intermediaries" that facilitate the ebb and flow of understandings between stakeholders. A computer-based simulation model then is seen explicitly as a tool to allow understandings of a problem situation to develop, to be discussed, and to be refined toward a solution.

1.3 *Applications in ongoing simulation modelling*

These examples show how computer technology (in the form of simulation models) has led us to a particular view of the role of technology in decision support. This view has enabled us to develop software which we suggest improves the process of communicating problem understandings. In the following sections, we look at some of the aims of computer-based simulation modelling as developed by the Centre for Applied Simulation Modelling (CASM) at the London School of Economics, and at Brunel University.

At the outset, it should be recognised that the process of problem communication itself and the nature of mental models are not areas in which we have any particular empirical research interests. Rather, we are interested in application techniques of computer-based simulation modelling -- in the ways that the process of simulation modelling can be facilitated through development of more sophisticated technology to communicate problem understandings.

2. Computer-based simulation modelling

2.1 *The traditional view of modelling process*

Simulation modelling is particularly popular amongst the operations research and information systems fraternities. Practitioners would offer the following description of the process of simulation modelling.

o   There is a real world problem.

o   This problem is formulated as a logical model in the form of activity cycle diagrams, flow charts, or block diagrams (amongst others). There are a variety of ways to represent the logic of the formulated problem.

o   The logical model is converted into a computer model (sometimes a computer program, other times a data driven generic simulation system).

o   This computer model is verified (tested to see if it is doing what the analyst wants it to do).

o   The model then is used as an operational model to produce some results or conclusions, or for implementation (after the operational model has been validated against the real world).

An implicit assumption in this process is that the product of modelling is a set of results (usually numerical) which lead decision makers and/or analysts to conclusions from which decisions are implemented.

2.2 *Our view of the modelling process*

However, our view of the process is somewhat different. First, in many real world situations problems are owned by interest groups (some of whom are in conflict). The

definition of the problem is influenced by the owners of the problem -- especially in complex strategic decision making.

Second, because the problem is complex, formulation of it is a difficult task. The construction of a logical model representing the formulation of the problem is, in many instances, the most difficult aspect of the problem treatment.

Third, understanding what the problem is may be the object of the entire exercise. This means that an analyst should be prepared to undertake problem reformulation constantly, in order to obtain a common understanding of the problem as part of the modelling process.

Finally, it needs to be possible to turn a dynamic logical model into a computer model with relative ease. If this part of the process takes a long time, contact with the real world problem starts to diminish. For example, if an analyst discusses the computer model with decision-makers infrequently, then the chance is small that the computer model will represent the real world problem adequately.

In many instances then, the computer model serves as a medium of communication for problem understandings, to all participants in the decision making process. Obviously, it is necessary to verify that the computer model does what one thinks it should. But it is questionable how much emphasis should be placed on generating an operational model for experimentation purposes. In many cases, the production of a computer model which succeeds in adequate problem definition agreement among decision-makers may be sufficient.

2.3 *Major issues and problems*

There are several issues and problems associated with using simulation modelling as a decision aiding technique. We have attempted to address these, partly based on our understanding of simulation models as a medium of communication.

First, most problems to which simulation applies are poorly defined. In fact, if the problem is not poorly defined there probably are better and more reliable methods of solving it than the rather crude technique of simulation modelling.

Second, any complex, important problem probably will involve conflicting interests and understandings. If the modelling process is going to lead to change, it is unlikely that all decision makers will see these changes as favourable to them. As much as possible, the modelling process should be used in a neutral way to help participants understand their problem.

Third, specification of "the problem" is never static. Even if one succeeds in satisfying the conflicting views of decision-makers, it is probable for complex problems that the specification will undergo change. The real world is dynamic. Therefore, the perceived problem will be dynamic.

The fourth problem is the question of "model confidence". No computer simulation of any size can possibly be verified; no model of any size can possibly be validated against the real world, given that the real world is not static.

A final and crucial feature of simulation modelling is that it involves "decision aiding". Discrete event simulation modelling is a quantitative technique. The outputs are numerical, and numerical values tend to indicate that one course of action might be better than another. However, such numerical techniques cannot represent all possible factors in the problem scenario. They can represent crudely most or some factors in a quantitative way, but they cannot represent subjective factors.

In our view then, the simulation modelling process is not designed to find "the answer". Rather, it aims to help participants make decisions or to understand a problem. It follows, therefore, that the development of computer systems for simulation modelling is driven by the need to make simulation efficient as a modelling tool, in order to help decision-makers understand their problems.

As a result, our primary concerns include:

o   to recognise the role of such tools in communicating understandings,

o   to provide methods by which computer-based tools can communicate those understandings effectively, and

o   to design tools so that analysts can develop simulations which embody problem understandings.

The following section discusses in greater detail the kinds of tools which we have developed to address these concerns.

3. Computer-based environments for simulation modelling

The essential feature of simulation modelling -- problem formulation and understanding -- has led us to develop computer-based tools which facilitate their role as dynamic intermediaries.

3.1 *Areas of development*

We have undertaken development in several areas: specification methods, problem formulators, and interactive visual simulations. It is this last area which we suggest is most effective in communicating problem understandings through technology. We briefly review all three, to highlight the differences among them.

SPECIFICATION METHODS

An essential part of simulation modelling is specifying the problem. If a specification is going to be used as a vehicle for communication, it must have a simple structure. However, many simulation models must represent complex situations: the combination of objects or of entities in an activity requires that some complex conditions be stated. If these conditions are described explicitly in the specification method, then the specification becomes difficult to follow.

There are several ways the problem can be specified, such as diagrammatic techniques (Ceric and Paul, 1989) -- including activity cycle diagrams and Petri nets, and semi-formal or mathematical methods (Zeigler, 1984). Paul and Ceric (1992) propose the principle of "Comprehensive Harmony" as a requirement for specification: the method must be reasonably comprehensive. However, comprehensiveness must be balanced by a harmony in the method that makes it intelligible to active participants in the simulation modelling process.

PROBLEM FORMULATORS

A problem formulator (Balmer and Paul, 1986) assists the analyst and decision-maker in formulating the nature of a problem. The system captures the model logic of the problem, then applies an interactive simulation program generator (ISPG). The ISPG produces a simulation model which calls a library of software subsystems to run the simulation itself. Simulation model output is analysed by an output analyser, which helps determine experimental designs for running and controlling the simulation model. The problem formulator and output analyser close the loop, so that the analyst and decision-makers collectively use the complete system. The Centre for Applied Simulation Modelling have made attempts to develop a problem formulator (Doukidis, 1985 and1987; Doukidis and Paul, 1987; Paul and Doukidis, 1986; Paul, 1987).

INTERACTIVE VISUAL SIMULATION

In an attempt to overcome these difficulties, CASM has developed tools for interactive visual simulation. These provide a dynamic and highly usable prototyping environment in which a problem owner and analyst can build a simulation model, in a collaborative manner.

Visual modelling is a powerful component of an analyst's problem-solving capabilities. Existing specification methods normally require a translation process between abstract psychological representation (the analyst's problem understanding) and the logical representation of the model (in terms of diagramming techniques or macro languages, for example).

Interactive visual simulation tools, on the other hand,

provide a simulation environment which enables constant reconstruction of the model -- by allowing the user to draw a visual representation of the real world system.

3.2 *Macintosh Graphical Simulation Environment (MacGraSE)*

A research system (MACGRASE) based on these observations and experiences was developed for the Apple Macintosh. (MACGRASE is primarily a demonstrator for the approach to visual interactive simulation and is available free of charge from CASM. Please contact Ray Paul (Ray.Paul@brunel.ac.uk)

MACGRASE was developed to investigate use of an environment which allows users to create a visual version of their understanding of the problem directly (during construction of the model), without being required first to translate the modeller's understandings into a logical structured form.

We shall describe briefly some features of the system.

It is clear that providing context for the decision-maker and for the analyst is an important part of formulating problems and communicating understanding using such a system. One way this can be accomplished is through use of simple visual elements, such as "fixed backgrounds" -- against which entities modelled in the system can be represented. A fixed background might take the form of a picture of the real world problem being modelled (the layout of a port, of a production line, or of an out-patient clinic, for example).

On the surface of the fixed background, graphical objects are used to represent entities in the simulation. In order to make the pictorial descriptions correspond to the real image of the system, each entity type has its own iconic representation. Model logic then can be defined by using the icons on the screen. Icons indicate *Entities* (any component of the model which can be imagined to retain its identity through time) and *Activities* (active states in which Entities of different types engage in cooperative tasks of some duration). The display of *Queues* (passive states of an Entity type while it waits for an Activity to commence) and *Attributes* (values or characteristics of each Entity) is optional. The way that Entities move about in the system forms the basic model logic.

The main advantage of using an application such as MACGRASE is its visual interface. This allows the user to have complete control over the application during construction of the simulation model. Moreover, the formulation mechanism allows the user to reconstruct the model continuously, throughout the model-building process. The tight indexing of Entity icons is so apparent that the user can modify an existing path or create an additional path easily, anywhere within their life cycle. For simulation models that are heavily attribute-based, the user can model the movements in attribute evaluation easily.

MACGRASE was prototyped with a facility to run the model interpretively, so that the analyst and the customer could see not only the visual image of the problem being modelled, but also the outcomes of current model construction. This facility is essential if the objective is to move as soon as possible towards a tight specification of the problem being modelled.

This iterative derivation of a model is in turn highly dependent on the speed with which the model can be adapted to meet new understandings. The MACGRASE prototype demonstrates that the visual approach is capable of the required speed. However, it is yet to be determined whether or not the level of functionality required of a production version would be greater. (Increased functionality might slow the tools' adaptation speed.)

The appropriate level of functionality is a balance between the need to make the system comprehensive enough for a wide range of problems, and the need to keep the system manageable. The existence of this tradeoff is one reason why we elected to incorporate a program generator into the prototype. The interpreted version of the model can manage the basic model structure, and allow for quick understanding. This first-cut model then can be expanded in the code-generated version, to include the extra detail considered necessary to advance use of the model. It is a positive side benefit that this style of model construction encourages the analyst to "grow the model" whilst retaining control of the understanding that is derived from the model.

4. Conclusions

We conceive of the use of computer-based simulation models to be essentially a process of applying technology to communicate problem understandings.

Our experience is that using tools such as MACGRASE (and other visual simulators) makes it possible to focus explicitly on the communication of problem understandings, in such a way that problems become more open to discussion, thereby allowing easier resolution.

Given that we have not been interested in this process primarily as an empirical phenomenon, we have little hard data about the detailed effectiveness of the computer tools we have developed. However, we suggest that studies of the use of systems such as MacGraSE (and of the use of computer-based simulation models in general) will validate the assertion that such tools can support the process of decision making effectively, by acting as dynamic intermediaries. We further suggest that computer-based simulation modelling represents a useful "laboratory" -- a laboratory in which we can seek to develop more comprehensive understandings of the ways in which mental models are used in real world settings.

References

BALMER, D. W. & PAUL, R. J. 1986, CASM -- The right environment for simulation. *Journal of the Operational Research Society* 37 (5), 443-452.

BELLOTTI, V. 1990, A framework for assessing applicability of HCI techniques. In D. Diaper et al (eds), *Proceedings of the Third IFIP TC13 Conference on Human-Computer Interaction, Interact'90*, 213-218. (North-Holland, Amsterdam).

BELLOTTI, V. 1988, Implications of current design practice for the use of HCI techniques. In D.M. Jones and R. Winder (eds), *People and Computers IV*, 13-34 (Cambridge University Press, Cambridge, UK).

BEWLAY, W. L., ROBERTS, T. L., SCHROIT, D. & VERPLANK, W. 1983, Human factors in the design of Xerox 8010 Star office workstation. *Human Factors in Computing Systems*, Proceedings of the CHI'83 Conference (Boston), 72-77 (ACM, New York).

BODKER, S. 1991, *Through the Interface* (Lawrence Erlbaum Associates, Hillsdale, NJ).

BRIGGS, P. 1988, What we know and what we need to know: the user model versus the user's model in human-computer interaction. *Behaviour and Information Technology* 7 (4), 431-442.

CARD, S. K., MORAN, T. P. & NEWELL, A. 1983, *The Psychology of Human-Computer Interaction.* (Lawrence Erlbaum Associates, Hillsdale, NJ).

CARROLL, J. M. & CARRITHERS C. 1984, Training wheels in a user interface. *Communications of the ACM* 27 (8), 800-806.

CARROLL, J. M. & OLSEN, J. R. 1988, Mental models in human-computer interaction. In. M. Helander (ed), *Handbook of Human-Computer Interaction*, 46-65 (Elsevier, Amsterdam).

CARROLL, J. M. & ROSSON, M. B. 1987, The Paradox of the active user. In J.M. Carroll (ed), *Interfacing Thought*, 80-111 (MIT Press, Cambridge, MA).

CERIC, V. & PAUL, R. J. 1989, Preliminary investigations into simulation model representation. In *Proceedings, 11th International Symposium on "Computer at the University"* (Cavtat, Yugoslavia, June).

CURTIS, B., KRASNER, H. & ISCOE, N. 1988, A field study of the software design process for large systems. *Communications of the ACM* 31 (11), 1268-1287.

DAGWELL, R. & WEBER, W. 1983, System designers' user models: A comparative study and methodological critique. *Communications of the ACM* 26, 987-997.

DOUKIDIS, G. I. 1987, An anthology on the homology of simulation with artificial intelligence. *Journal of the Operational Research Society* 38 (8)(August), 701-712.

DOUKIDIS, G. I. 1985, Discrete Event Simulation Model Formulation Using Natural Language Understanding Systems. Unpublished Ph.D thesis. (University of London, England).

DOUKIDIS, G. I. & PAUL, R. J. 1987, Artificial intelligence aids in discrete event digital simulation modelling. In *IEE Proceedings* 134, Pt.D (4)(July), 278-286.

DUBOULAY, B., O'SHEA, T. & MONK, J. 1981, The black box inside the glass box: Presenting computing concepts to novices. *International Journal of Man-Machine Studies* 14, 237-249.

EL-SHEIKH, A., PAUL, R. J., HARDING, A. S. & BALMER, D. W. 1987, A microcomputer-based simulation study of a port. *Journal of the Operational Research Society* 38 (8), 673-681.

FAROOQ, M. U. & DOMINICK, W. D. 1988, A survey of formal tools and models for developing user interfaces. International *Journal of Man-Machine Studies* 29, 479-496.

FISCHER, G. 1991, The importance of models in making complex systems comprehensible. In M. J. Tauber & D. Ackerman (eds), *Mental Models and Human-Computer Interaction 2* (North-Holland, Amsterdam).

GENTNER, D. & STEVENS, A. L. (eds) 1983, *Mental Models* (Lawrence Erlbaum Associates, Hillsdale, NJ).

GOULD, J. D. & LEWIS, C. 1985, Designing for usability -- key principles and what designers think. *Communications of the ACM* 28, 300-311.

GOULD, J. D., BOIES, S. J., LEVY, S., RICHARDS, J. T. & SCHOONARD, J. 1987, The 1984 Olympic Games messaging system: A test of behavioural principles of system design. *Communications of the ACM* 30, 785-796.

HALASZ, F. G. & MORAN, T. P. 1983, Mental models and problem- solving in using a calculator. *Human Factors in Computing Systems*, Proceedings of the CHI'83 Conference, Boston, 212- 216. New York: Association for Computing Machinery.

HAMMOND, N., JORGENSEN, A., MACLEAN, A., BARNARD, P. & LONG, J. 1983, Design practice and interface usability: Evidence from interviews with designers. *Human Factors in Computing Systems*, Proceedings of the CHI'83 Conference (Boston, December), 40- 44 (ACM, New York).

HEATH, C. & LUFF, P. 1991, Disembodied conduct: communication through video in a multi-media office environment. *Human Factors in Computing Systems*, Proceedings of the CHI'91 Conference, 99-103 (ACM, New York).

JOHNSON, P. & NICOLOSI, E. 1990, Task-based user interface development tools. In D. Diaper et al (eds), *Proceedings of the Third IFIP TC13 Conference on Human-Computer Interaction Interact'90*, 383-387 (North-Holland, Amsterdam).

JOHNSON-LAIRD, P. N. 1983, *Mental Models* (Cambridge University Press, Cambridge, UK).

LANDAUER, T. K. 1987, Relations between cognitive psychology and computer system design. In J. M. Carroll (ed), *Interfacing Thought*, 1-25 (MIT Press, Cambridge, MA).

LANG, K. N., AULD, R., & LANG, T. 1982, The goals and methods of computer-users. *International Journal of Man-Machine Studies* 17, 375-399.

LAWRENCE, D., ATWOOD, M., DEWS, S. & TURNER, T. 1995 Social interaction in the design and use of a workstation: Two contexts of interaction. In P. Thomas (ed), *The Social and Interactional Dimensions of Human-Computer Interface,* 240-259 (Cambridge University Press, Cambridge, UK).

LEWIS, C. 1986, Understanding what's happening in system interactions. In D. A. Norman & S. W. Draper (eds), *User Centred System Design*, 169-185 (Lawrence Erlbaum Associates, Hillsdale, NJ).

LUFF, P., FROHLICH, D. & GILBERT, G. (eds) 1990, *Computers and Conversation* (Academic Press, London).

McLEAN, A., BELLOTTI, V. & YOUNG, R. 1990, What rationale is there in design. In D. Diaper et al (eds), *Proceedings, Third IFIP TC13 Conference on Human-Computer Interaction Interact'90*, 207-212. North Holland, Amsterdam).

NICKERSON, R. S. 1976, On conversational interaction with computers. In R.M. Baecker & W.A.S. Buxton (eds) 1987), *Readings in Human Computer Interaction*, 681-693 (Morgan Kaufmann, Los Altos, CA).

NORMAN, D. A. 1988, *The Psychology of Everyday Things* (Basic Books, New York).

NORMAN, D. A. 1987, Cognitive artifacts. In J. M. Carroll (ed), *Interfacing Thought*, 17-38 (MIT Press, Cambridge, MA).

NORMAN, D. A. 1983, Some observations on mental models. In D. Gentner & A. Stevens (eds), *Mental Models* (Lawrence Erlbaum Associates, Hillsdale, NJ).

NORMAN, M. A. & THOMAS, P. J. 1990, The very idea: Informing HCI design from conversation analysis. In P. Luff et al (eds), *Computers and Conversation*, 51-65 (Academic Press, London).

PAUL, R. J. 1993, Why users cannot get what they want. In *Proceedings, the Do Users Get What They Want Conference* (Centre for Research into Innovation, Culture and Technology, Brunel University).

PAUL, R. J. 1991, Recent developments in simulation modelling. *Journal of the Operational Research Society* 42 (3), 217-226.

PAUL, R. J. 1987, A.I. and stochastic process simulation. In B. Phelps (ed), *Interactions in Artificial Intelligence and Statistical Methods*, 85-98 (Gower Technical Press, London).

PAUL, R. J. & CERIC, V. 1992, Methods of Model Representation in Discrete Event Simulation: An Overview. Submitted to *Transactions of The Society for Modelling and Computer Simulation.*

PAUL, R. J. & DOUKIDIS, G. I. 1986, Further developments in the use of artificial intelligence techniques which formulate simulation problems. *Journal of the Operational Research Society* 37 (8)(August).

RANDALL, D. & HUGHES, J. 1995, Working with customers: CSCW and office work. In P. Thomas (ed), *The Social and Interactional Dimensions of Human-Computer Interface,* 142-160 (Cambridge University Press, Cambridge, UK).

RILEY, M. 1986, User understanding. In D. A. Norman & S. W. Draper (eds), *User Centred System Design*, 157-169 (Lawrence Erlbaum Associates, Hillsdale, NJ).

SUCHMAN, L. A. 1987, *Plans and Situated Actions: The problem of Human-Computer Communication* (Cambridge University Press, Cambridge, UK).

THOMAS, P. (ed) 1995, *Personal Information Systems: Business Applications* (Stanley Thomas, Cheltenham).

WINOGRAD, T. 1987, A language/action perspective on the design of cooperative work. *Human Computer Interaction* 3, 3-30.

ZEIGLER, B. P. 1984, *Multifacetted Modelling and Discrete Event Modelling* (Academic Press, London).

8

The effects of combining interactive graphics and text in computer-mediated small group decision-making

JOZSEF TOTH

Learning Research & Development Center, University of Pittsburgh, 3939 O'Hara Street, Room 561, Pittsburgh, PA 15260 USA
jtoth+@pitt.edu

Abstract. Research in computer-mediated small group tasks has focused primarily on the medium of sentential messages. This chapter details exploratory research which instead combines a synchronous sentential messaging medium with two-dimensional interactive graphics.

Eleven three-person groups participated in a risk-taking, choice-dilemma task involving collection of prediscussion opinions, discussion of the choice-dilemma, consensus attainment, and collection of postdiscussion opinions. Two conditions, one in which groups selected and received feedback of their graphics-based prediscussion opinions {g}, and a second, which also included a graphical representation of the prediscussion average {g+avg}, were coupled with a sentential communication medium. A third sentential-only {s} condition served as a control.

In the condition with the graphical prediscussion opinions and average {g+avg}, groups sent proportionately more messages making persuasive arguments and proportionately fewer messages proposing values and unsubstantiated opinion about the group decision. In the graphical condition without the average {g}, the reverse effect was observed. In the control {s}, the same discussion parameters fell proportionately between the two graphics conditions. In both graphics conditions, the first advocate had a stronger influence on the group decision than in the control. The data suggest that the inclusion of two-dimensional graphics can either facilitate or inhibit normative and informational forms of social influence during the group decision-making process.

1. Introduction

Investigation into how the use of computers can affect group and organisational behaviour has burgeoned in the past decade. By comparing factors between face-to-face (FF) and computer-mediated (CM) small groups, significant computer-mediation effects have been discovered.

These effects typically result from synchronous discussion programs or the transmission of asynchronous electronic mail messages. In such cases, the members of CM small groups (comprising 2, 3 or 4 people) have been isolated from each other verbally and nonverbally, so that their only means of communication has been through computer mediation. Significant CM effects include:

o   the temporal duration of discussion is increased,

o   the effects on the group decision due to members' high and low status are equalised,

o   the influence on the group decision of the group member who first advocates a decision proposal is attenuated,

o   individual participation in the group discussion is equalised, and

o   the shift between the aggregate opinions held by group members before, during and after discussions is exaggerated.

(see Kiesler & Sproull, 1992, for a review)

Throughout most of this work, it has been argued that the removal of vital *social context cues* under CM conditions has either exacerbated or attenuated various social psychological phenomena within groups. The tasks used in such research have primarily involved decision-making. However, the broader implications of findings bear ultimately on the everyday and widespread organisational use of computers. For instance, if a geographically disparate group conducts a good part of its communication and decision-making activity through electronic mail, what are the gross implications for the overall efficacy or quality of such a group's decisions -- as compared to those of an organisation whose activities transpire primarily in face-to-face settings?

The *modality* in this computer-mediated research to date has involved only *sentential* text (i.e., that organised as human language sentences). The primary focus of this chapter will be to extend and refine the notion of computer-mediation to include two-dimensional interactive computer graphics.

There are three primary concerns motivating this inquiry.

First, the wholesale use of low-cost, interactive, graphics-based, networked computer workstations is on the rise. Thus, it is not uncommon for networked group activity to include the integration of graphics and text.

Second, if the use of computer-mediated sentential text has been found to have such a wide variety of effects on small-group behaviour, what added effects might the combination of interactive text *and* graphics have on groups? By integrating discourse-based sentential text with two-dimensional interactive computer graphics, this chapter will demonstrate that there are indeed significant effects when the two are combined.

Finally, if significant differences are to be found among communication modalities that extend beyond sentential text, what are the implications for the designers *and* users of such systems in coming years?

This exposition will focus primarily on how the differences in communication modalities affect group members' attempts to *influence* each other in the course of decision-making discussion.

2. Theoretical background

It would be highly desirable if the cognitive sciences had developed comprehensive and integrated theories of attention, perception and cognition, plus associated theories concerning the effective design and use of information displays. At present, however, only fragments exist. In this section, two sub-disciplines will be reviewed in order to frame the ensuing empirical analysis and discussion. These sub-disciplines are (a) cognitive-perceptual efficiency and salience, and (b) small group processes involving influence and decision-making.

2.1 *Cognitive-perceptual efficiency and salience*

One theoretical assumption latent in the research described later is the acknowledgment that there are fundamental differences in the way humans perceive and understand spoken and written language, on the one hand,

and how they apprehend non-language visual information, on the other. This assumption bears on the differences between the modalities of sentential text and two-dimensional (2D) interactive computer graphics -- and how these differences might be utilised effectively in the design of human-computer interfaces for computer-mediated small groups.

The intrinsic properties of these two modalities -- and how they bear on human attention, perception and cognition -- still are widely contested topics. For instance, written (e.g., sentential) and spoken language are presumed to share the same phonological component (Van Orden et al, 1990). However, no one has been able to determine whether sentential information is manipulated internally and represented as a canonical semantic structure -- a structure which also represents information from other non-language modalities (Kaplan & Simon, 1989).

This chapter does not seek to answer such questions. Rather, it assumes that the semantics of various modalities -- visual, verbal, written, etc. -- must somehow *interact* within and between various internal modes of processing. For instance, reading the written word DOG not only evokes a phonological activation of the spoken word "DOG", but also elicits dog-related mental images and sounds (e.g., barking, whining; Paivio, 1986).

Moreover, in problems that are *isomorphic* (Kotovsky et al, 1985; Zhang & Norman, 1990), the manner in which each type of problem is presented to the problem solver yields widely disparate response times, levels of performance and comprehension (Lewis & Toth, 1992; Tabachnek & Simon 1992).

A common theme permeating the work in problem isomorphs suggests that language-based representations consume more cognitive resources and are more prone to the effects of working memory (Schneider & Detweiler, 1987). By contrast, when consistently mapped, non-language visual representations result in resource-free and highly automatic modes of processing. Such modes are much more impervious to the effects of working memory, and possess a high degree of cognitive impenetrability. By "non-language", I mean ecologically available visual information that appeals to nomic visual processing and which has enjoyed a genetic advantage over spoken and written language by at least a few hundred million years. By "consistently mapped", I mean the work first detailed by Shiffrin & Schneider (1977) in which the choice and layout of stimuli had an extremely profound effect on whether controlled or automatic attentive and perceptual processing occurred. This paradigm was later extended to involve certain forms of cognitive processing, as well, in a chess context (Fisk & Lloyd, 1988).

In the realm of text processing and comprehension, similar findings have been noted. For instance, the comprehension of text has been known to conflict with the reader's inferences and background knowledge, leading to inferences that were not part of the original text (Bransford, Barclay, & Franks, 1972). In other cases, it has been demonstrated that subjects erroneously "remember" aspects or details of a story that were not present in the original text (Loftus, Miller, & Burns, 1978). Regarding the understanding of non-linguistic information, similar results have been obtained in the understanding of novel and permuted stimuli (Mandler & Ritchey, 1977; Nickerson & Adams, 1979).

One ramification of this consistently mapped phenomenon is an implication that the stimuli (or salient aspects of the stimuli) inherently possess the potential to be available for effortless, internal processing -- even in the *absence* of the original stimulus (just as is possible in certain forms of imagery). For example, keeping one's eyes closed, sustaining a mental image of the Towers of Hanoi problem, and then solving it, is quite within the realm of such nomic processing. It is argued that such "envisionment" is much more difficult to accomplish for spoken and written language with respect to the *original* stimuli. In other words, solving a sentential version of the Towers of Hanoi (e.g., "the large disk and the small disk are on the middle peg and the medium disk is on the left peg") would be next to impossible.

Unfortunately, what continues to evade cognitive scientists is a lawfully articulated set of principles and guidelines for the organisation of such theoretical building-blocks into an ontology that then can be utilised by the applied sciences. For example, it couldn't have been predicted by most theories of the time that the radial-spatial aspects of the analogue fuel, temperature and velocity gauges (rather than the digital-numerical incarnations of the same) would present less of a hindrance to the motorist who must divide attention between the road ahead and the instrument display below. Sometimes, only trial-and-error can be trusted to establish what is effective and what isn't.

Relating to the work reported in this paper, the *semantic* impact of the use of one modality rather than another in terms of working memory limitations is of particular interest, as is how both modalities interact in the course of perception and cognition. If one modality (language) is more resource-bounded and the other (non-language) is more resource-free (i.e., non-language), and if the information conveyed is isomorphic (e.g., the written number 9 versus the x or y position of 9 on a 2D graph), it is hypothesised that the resource-free representation will have more of an influence on cognitive processing which takes such information into account. It also is argued that this effect can persist even after removal of the original stimulus, when such a stimulus entails resource-free processing.

2.2 *Influence and decision-making in small groups*

When FF and CM small groups engage in discourse-based decision-making, the typical task performed is of the risk-taking *judgmental* variety, for which no absolute or correct answer exists. An example of such a problem, known as a *choice-dilemma*, follows.

> Ms. H, a college senior, has studied the piano since childhood. She has won amateur prizes and given small recitals, suggesting that Ms. H has considerable musical talent. As graduation approaches, Ms. H has the choice of going to medical school to become a physician, a profession which would bring certain prestige and financial rewards; or entering a conservatory of music for advanced training with a well-known pianist. Ms. H realises that even upon completion of her piano studies, which would take many more years and a lot of money, success as a concert pianist would not be assured.

> Keep in mind that the riskier alternative, entering a conservatory of music, is always assumed to be more desirable than the safer course, going to medical school.

When an experimental group is presented such a problem, members are asked to discuss the choice dilemma and to arrive at a consensus that reflects their aggregate advice to the central character, Ms. H. This advice is articulated as a single risk value ranging from 1-in-10 to 9-in-10, where 1-in-10 is riskiest and 9-in-10 is safest. This value reflects the lowest probability of success that the group would consider acceptable in order for Ms. H to give the risky alternative a try. Before the discussion begins and after the discussion ends, each member is asked to state, in isolation from the rest of the group, what advice should be given. When discussion begins, each member has a preconceived notion of what the *consensus* value should be. Since individuals' values seldom are in agreement at the onset of discussion, members must adjust their initial positions as the discussion proceeds and as the group consensus evolves.

Many theories have been advanced to explain both the phenomena during decision-making discussions, and how group members compel each other to change positions. Two of the most popular theories entail influence and decision rules.

There are two varieties of influence: normative and informational (Ridgeway, 1984). *Normative influence* centers on social norms, and how group members adhere to such norms in order to influence each others' behaviour and thoughts. To sway a differing opinion, this type of influence can be as "primal" as brow-beating and shouting, or it can be more implicit and culturally embedded in social class, gender or accepted social protocol (such as the influence of the majority). *Informational influence,* by contrast, is more "cerebral" in nature, in that it requires discussants to employ persuasive arguments that are grounded in fact, logic and inference in order to argue for or against a particular position.

Finally, *decision rules*, which may include aspects of normative and informational influence, are analytical heuristics developed by social scientists. Sometimes they can predict a group decision reliably, given members' prediscussion opinions (Miller, 1989). One such rule is *majority wins*: if a prediscussion majority exists (e.g., 1-in-10, 2-in-10, 9-in-10), the group decision (e.g., 3-in-10) will tend towards the majority position. In this particular decision rule, the coercion of the majority implies a normative style of influence. Another such rule is the *average rule*, which typically occurs when there is an even distribution of opinion (e.g., 1-in-10, 5-in-10, 9-in-10). The group either quickly or as the result of an impasse decides to take the average of their opinions (e.g., 5-in-10). This decision rule is more grounded in the notion of informational influence.

3. Hypotheses tested

The principal empirical parameter in exploratory work reported in this chapter is the opinions group members hold individually about the central character's dilemma, before discussion begins (e.g., their initial "advice" to Ms. H). Historically, such prediscussion opinions -- as well as opinions established early in discussion (realised as decision proposals) -- are known to have significant effects on discussion outcome, or on group consensus. Varying the modality of prediscussion opinions should affect subsequent reasoning markedly, in the ensuing discussion phase. The modality being explored may be more resource-bounded (sentential text) or more resource-free (2D graphics).

Since a resource-free presentation of prediscussion opinions involves visual information that is more salient and persistent, it is argued here that such information can sustain a ten minute discussion -- even in the *absence* of the original stimulus -- and significantly affect group members' reasoning. Bearing in mind what has been discussed regarding the way group members seek to influence each others' opinions, it can be expected that salient information captured in the 2D graphical representation will direct the group's reasoning and discussion. Regarding group behaviour, this effect may be rendered either in terms of normative or information influence.

Two graphical representations were created to test the postulated effects. The first was a mapping of three individual choice-dilemma prediscussion opinions onto a standard two-dimensional graph, whereby risk value corresponded to the spatial *y* aspect of the graph {g}. The second type was identical in composition to the first, but also included a graphical representation of the prediscussion average {g+avg}. Three hypotheses were established regarding {g} and {g+avg}, with a third sentential-only representation (no graphics) serving as control {s}. The experimental design is summarised in Tables 1 and 2.

Table 1.   Summary of anticipated findings, group consensus hypotheses (H1, H3)

		Treatment conditions (IVs)					
		No first advocacy			First advocacy		
		g	g+avg	s	g	g+avg	s
Level of accord (averaging effect, DVs)	**high**		x		x	x	
	medium	x					
	low						x
	none		x				

Note: "x" indicates level of anticipated finding for treatment indicated

H1.   INDIVIDUAL AND GROUP OPINION

It was predicted that the value of the group consensus would be most in accord with {g+avg}. The average, as such, would imply an informational, mathematically derived "consensus" which the group would be compelled to adopt. The mode {g} also was expected to have an averaging effect on group consensus, but this effect was not expected to be as great as that for {g+avg}, since the average would be implicit (it would not necessarily be derived during group discussions). In sum, the two graphics-based displays {g} and {g+avg} were expected to attenuate the *choice shift* phenomenon (measured as the average of absolute values of differences between individual prediscussion opinions and the consensus). It was predicted that {s} would have no average effect; that instead it would induce the choice shift noted in earlier work (Siegel et al, 1986).

H2.   GROUP DISCUSSION

Since {g+avg} contained encapsulated, cohesive information about the group (i.e., prediscussion opinions summarised as the average), it was predicted that discussants would voice more informational influence content and less normative influence content than in {g} or {s}. It also was predicted that the duration of discussion would be briefer and that discussion content would be more concise in {g+avg}, compared to {g} or {s}. (Subjects would arrive quickly at the consensus implied by the prediscussion graphical average.)

Regarding {g}, discussants were expected to use less

Table 2.   Summary of anticipated findings, group discussion hypotheses (H2)

Level of influence

		Treatment conditions		
		g	g+avg	s
Normative (opinion)	high	x		
	medium			x
	low		x	
Informational (persuasion)	high	x		
	medium			x
	low	x		

Length of discussion

	Treatment conditions		
	g	g+avg	s
high			x
medium	x		
low		x	

Conciseness of content

	Treatment conditions		
	g	g+avg	s
high		x	
medium	x		
low			x

Note: "x" indicates level of anticipated finding for treatment indicated

informational influence and more normative influence, compared to {g+avg} or {s}. (Absence of a group prediscussion average would promote lack of cohesion in aggregate opinion, reinforcing individual opinion evidenced by a more normative influence.) Discussion in {g} was predicted to be briefer and more concise than in {s}.

Faced with {s}, it was predicted that subjects would spend more time in discussion. (Group members would have to articulate their prediscussion opinions sententially, at the onset of discussion.)

H3. FIRST ADVOCACY

Two forms of first advocacy were considered: explicit and implicit. The interpretation of *explicit first advocate* follows the canonical definition used in computer-mediated and face-to-face research (Weisband, 1992; McGuire et al, 1987). This definition specifies that the first person make a specific, numerical decision proposal during the discussion phase (e.g., "I think it should be 1-in-10").

With inclusion of the graphical modality, a second type (*implicit first advocate*) specifies that an individual posts his/her opinion graphically, but does not explicitly articulate the value of that opinion during discussion. (For example, the individual does not say "I think he should go for it" during the discussion phase, after having selected a graphic value of 1-in-10 during the prediscussion phase.) In the case of {s}, the implicit first advocate would be referring to the opinion that s/he selected on the prediscussion questionnaire.

It was predicted that in {g} and {g+avg}, the first explicit or implicit advocate would have a stronger influence on the group consensus than in {s}. The source of this influence would stem from coupling cognitively and perceptually salient visual information with a subsequent reference to that information in the discussion. In the case of {s}, it was predicted that the first explicit or implicit advocate would have the least influence on group consensus, thereby replicating results of earlier CM research (Weisband, 1992).

4. Method

4.1 Design

To examine these projected effects, a pilot study was conducted. The within-group, repeated-measures experimental design was comprised of one independent variable (representational modality of group prediscussion opinions), and three conditions:

{s}: Prediscussion opinions were articulated in the sentential (text) modality by group members as their discussions began. This served both as a control condition and as an attempt to replicate results from earlier CM research.

{g}: Computer 2D graphical feedback of the group's pre-discussion opinions was provided to group members directly before discussions began.

{g+avg}: Computer 2D graphical feedback {g}, with addition of the prediscussion average provided to group members directly before discussions began.

4.2 *Subjects*

Subjects were 33 University of Pittsburgh students (18 men and 15 women, of varying ages and academic accomplishment). These individuals were assigned to 11 groups of 3 members each. Five groups included two females and one male; five groups consisted of two males and one female; the final group contained three males. Gender selection criteria were not expected to confound data. (Straus, 1991, found that the effects of gender in CM groups working on judgmental tasks were not significant.)

4.3 *Procedure*

At the beginning of the session, each group met face-to-face with the experimenter. Group members then were seated individually at Sun Microsystems Sparcstations with chromatic monitors. Two subjects were located in the same room, but were approximately 20 feet apart and were separated physically by two office partitions, ensuring verbal and non-verbal isolation. The third subject was seated in an adjacent room, separated from the other two subjects by a concrete wall, again ensuring isolation.

All software described below -- with the exception of the Internet Relay Chat (IRC) program -- was implemented using an X Windows-based graphics package and was developed in the Unix-based Sun Openwindows graphical display environment. The workstations were connected on a local area network. Each workstation was equipped with a keyboard, a three-button mouse and a pencil (to complete prediscussion and postdiscussion questionnaires). Further details of the configuration, and a sample workstation display, are available from the author.

The session consisted of one practice trial and three experimental trials -- one for each experimental condition. The practice trial always was first. The three experimental conditions were ordered in 3! combinations, totaling six possible sessions. Five combinations were performed by two groups each. Since there were 11 groups, the only order performed by one group was {g+avg} -- {g} -- {s}. Session duration ranged from 60-to-100 minutes.

The experimental trial, following the classical small group experimental paradigm (McGuire et al, 1987), was partitioned into four sequence-invariant phases:

(i) collection of individual prediscussion opinions,
(ii) group discussion,
(iii) group consensus attainment, and
(iv) collection of individual postdiscussion opinions.

The computer workstation display was partitioned by software into four like-sized windows. It followed the ``What You See is What I See'' (WYSIWIS) interface design philosophy.

An *Instruction* window at the upper left informed members of the group of what they should do next.

A graphics-based *Feedback* window at the upper right (for {g} and {g+avg} only), allowed subjects to select prediscussion, consensus and postdiscussion opinions with the three-button mouse. It also displayed aggregate opinions. Any of the three buttons on the mouse performed the same function when selecting a graphical item.

A *Problem* window at the lower left displayed the choice-dilemma problem. For {s}, the problem was "Ms. H" (see below). For {g}, the problem was a college graduate facing the choice of a difficult or an easy Ph.D. program. For {g+avg}, the central character (played by the subject) had to choose between staying with a lifelong career at a large firm or moving to a risky, yet potentially lucrative start-up company.

A *Discussion* window at the lower right, running the Internet Relay Chat (IRC) program, allowed subjects to type synchronous messages to each other during the discussion phase (ii). Text scrolled from bottom to top as the discussion proceeded, so that discussants could see prior statements made by others.

The experimenter was seated at a fourth workstation, which ran IRC and connected to the other three workstations, so that individual opinions could be collected electronically and stored to disk during {g} and {g+avg}. For instance, when collecting prediscussion opinions via mouse through the feedback window, the server recorded opinions from all three subjects. Then, it would broadcast the three opinions back to each subject's workstation. When each workstation received the broadcast, it would update the feedback window and display the group's opinions in a format consistent with either experimental condition {g} or {g+avg}. This collect/broadcast loop was kept the same for the consensus and postdiscussion phases in {g} and {g+avg}.

All mouse selections in the feedback window and keystrokes in the discussion window were recorded locally (on each workstation) for later analysis. Each message that a subject typed in IRC was prepended with an unique time-stamp, denoting minutes and seconds. Subjects were aware that the experimenter was viewing the discussion, and that their responses were being recorded. They were allowed to ask any procedural questions during the practice trial. Occasionally, procedural questions were asked during the experimental trials, but this typically occurred instead at the end of the discussion (e.g, "What do we do next?").

For the control condition {s} prediscussion phase (i), a questionnaire was distributed to each group member. Then, the member read the dilemma involving the central character and his risky/safe alternatives. Next, the members provided their individual written opinions. After the completed questionnaires were collected by the experimenter, in phase (ii) the group was instructed to discuss the problem using the IRC program. The instructions they read were as follow:

> Imagine that as a group, the three of you are advising Ms. H. Your task is to discuss Ms. H's dilemma and decide on the lowest probability that you would consider acceptable for Ms. H to continue with her musical training.
>
> Your group decision should consist of a single value ranging from 1-in-10 (riskiest) to 9-in-10 (safest).

The group was permitted to discuss the problem for as long as necessary to attain consensus. A timer in the feedback window displayed the number of minutes elapsed in the conversation. Once consensus was attained in (iii), the experimenter again distributed questionnaires to the group members.

The {g} and {g+avg} trials varied from the {s} trial in two important ways.

(a) Instead of written questionnaires, prediscussion (i), consensus (iii) and postdiscussion (iv) subjects selected opinions interactively from the feedback window, via the three-button mouse. The nine *y* axis labels, "1-in-10" through "9-in-10", could be selected by positioning the mouse pointer over the item and clicking a mouse button.

(b) Directly before the discussion began, the group viewed their prediscussion opinions in the Feedback Window. Each subject's name was enclosed in a graphical box and shown along the *y* position in the display, to the right of the *y* axis that corresponded to his/her prediscussion opinion. The *x* and *y* axes met at a common "origin". The *y* axis contained 9 hash marks, to denote each of the 9 discrete risk values. If two (or all three) subjects had the same opinion, the boxes were located at the same *y* position and were concatenated in alphabetical order. Boxes always were represented with the width of the longest subject-name, so that boxes would be the same size. (Potentially different box sizes would not confound results, by implying the "importance" of one opinion over another.)

For {g}, only opinions were displayed. {g+avg} was identical to {g}, except that the average of subjects' prediscussion opinions also was displayed, along with the numerical value of that average. If that value was non-discrete (e.g., 2.3), it was displayed as a *y* axis label. For both displays, the *x* position of boxes in the graph was held constant.

The displays in {g} and {g+avg} were presented to subjects for 90 seconds, then removed before the discussion phase (ii) began. As a result, the displays during the discussion phase essentially were the same for all three conditions. This sequencing was considered carefully, since it was hypothesised that any effects of prediscussion modality would appear during the discussion. Introducing additional interactive graphics during the discussion phase would have only confounded anticipated effects, and could have resulted in an undesired interaction effect between the prediscussion and discussion phases.

In {g} and {g+avg}, after the consensus value was selected (iii) the value was displayed to subjects again in the Feedback Window, for 45 seconds. The value was displayed as before, except that the subjects' graphical boxes were concatenated and ordered alphabetically at the *y* position, reflecting the group decision. In one case, the group agreed on a non-discrete value (e.g., 2.33), therefore they were not able to select the appropriate consensus value. The practice trial was identical to {g}, except that some instructions were more verbose.

5. Dependent measures and results

5.1 *Content coding*

For the 33 trials, duration of discussion, number of utterances, and prediscussion consensus and postdiscussion opinions were evaluated. Unique codes were edited into the data files using the Gnu Emacs text editor. A parser written in Lucid Lisp then was used to extract and tabulate the coded information.

In contrast with earlier CM work, the conversational unit of analysis in this study was defined as each subject's *message* in the IRC medium -- even if one message comprised two or three sentences. Most messages, no matter how long, typically carried one basic semantic theme or idea. In two cases, one {s} and one {g+avg}, single messages were partitioned into two separate messages, since they entailed semantic ideas which were irrefutably distinct.

The discussions in this experiment took on three salient characteristics that appeared consistently in all 33 discussions, reflecting a common discourse *structure*. Subjects spent their discussion time in one of three registers:

(a) Arguing or weighing the dilemma (the risky alternative against the safe alternative), in turn providing persuasive arguments for or against either alternative -- usually to support or refute a proposed consensus value. At times, such arguments were accompanied by a consensus proposal. Hereafter, this discourse type will be referred to as *persuasive arguments*.

(b) Proposing various values for the group consensus, sometimes accompanied by social pressure and/or unsubstantiated claims. Hereafter, this discourse type will be referred to as *normative arguments*.

(c) Settling on and affirming the consensus value. This activity ended all 33 discussions. Hereafter, this discourse type will be referred to as *consensus attainment*.

With few exceptions, all three registers occurred in contiguous sequences. For instance, in a few messages subjects weighed the risky and safe alternatives, then switched to proposing various consensus values, then made substantive arguments for or against their proposals, then finally came to agreement. For the purposes of this discussion, these contiguous sequences are recognised as distinct discourse *types*. More detailed examples of these types follow:

EXAMPLE 1

This sample is from a {g+avg} trial and is a superlative example of *persuasive arguments*:

<s0>   If it doesn't work out he is qualified enough [then] it should be relatively easy for him to find employment elsewhere.

<s1>   I disagree that jobs would be easy for him to find... it's a rough job market.

<s0>   But then again, is this scenario set during a recession or during a good economic period??

<s1>   What's the current economy? Who can tell?

<s0>   I am assuming that the scenario is time-invariant.

<s2>   With a degree in EE and 5 years experience, he can find a job.

<s1>   I've got friends with the same experience who are unemployed!

<s0>   Exactly.

<s0>   It may take a few months or a year (to find a new job).

<s2>   I would say again that one has to take risks in life.

<s0>   Anyway, assuming that the scenario is time-invariant the current conditions of the economy should not matter much.

EXAMPLE 2

This next example, from a {g} trial, demonstrates the interplay between (a) *normative arguments*, in which a majority-style normative pressure is applied, and (b) *persuasive arguments* (author's comments enclosed in parentheses).

<s1>   Let's go with 5-in-10.

<s0>   I've changed my mind. 2-in-10. What do you think?

<s2>   I say 2-in-10.

<s0>   Come on [s1].

<s2>   I think [s1] is being difficult.

<s1>   Tell me one reason why I should agree with you guys.

<s0>   Just as you said before, "If she puts her mind to it"! (majority-style normative pressure doesn't work, so switch to persuasive arguments)

<s2>   Why did you come to school here. You had a very good chance of success at a community college, but chose the tougher school. Why?

<s2>   Why? (continue on to consensus attainment)

<s1>   Okay, 2-in-10 (s1 acquiesces and the group reaches a decision).

EXAMPLE 3

This example is from an {s} trial. It includes a typical exchange, as discussion begins. The second utterance, by s1, is an instance of an *explicit decision proposal*.

<s2>   What is your choice on Ms. H?

<s1>   3-in-10.

<s2>   Remember, what are the lowest odds you would accept?

<s2>   I went with 8-in-10.

<s1>   3-in-10 is really risky. I would still take a chance.

EXAMPLE 4

These are opening utterances from a {g+avg} trial. They are a splendid example of an *implicit decision proposal*. S2 has selected 6-in-10, s1 7-in-10, and s0 2-in-10. Note how s1 and s2 discuss their opinions, as well as s0's opinion, without ever explicitly mentioning the value of these opinions. They instead refer to the graphical display, which they had seen initially and which is no longer present.

<s2>   The way the economy is today, I wouldn't take too many risks.

<s2>   I'm waiting to hear from you two.

<s1>   I don't like living in fear for the future of my kid

<s1>   I think you are right [s2].

<s2>   [s0] that is some kind of risk there. Why?

Later in the discussion, as consensus begins to coalesce, the first explicit advocacy appears.

<s2>   I will move to 5-in-10, and that's it!

<s2>   [s0] what say you?

<s0>   Well [s2], I'll do the same.

EXAMPLE 5

Finally, this example illustrates what happens typically during *consensus attainment*.

<s1>   I COULD GO WITH 4-IN-10.
<s0>   Have we decided?
<s2>   Okay, then it is in agreement with 4-in-10.
<s0>   Yes.
<s1>   Yes, 4-in-10.

5.2 *Statistical results*

From hypotheses H1, H2 and H3, seven dependent measures were analysed for statistical significance, using one-way analysis of variance (Table 3).

For the three experimental conditions, there was no significant difference in discussion duration. The choice shift between the average of prediscussion opinions and group consensus was not significant. Attitude polarisation, or the shift between the prediscussion average and postdiscussion average, also was not significant. The lack of a choice shift is not consistent with earlier sentential CM research (Siegel et al, 1986).

The *degree* of shift, however, is considerably greater compared with that observed in earlier research. For instance, Siegel found mean choice shift for synchronous computer-mediated discussion to be .89. Since that study used a completely different discussion medium (it was terminal and mainframe-based rather than workstation-based), it is not prudent to suggest what additional factors might have led to these differences between studies.

H1. INDIVIDUAL AND GROUP OPINION

The first hypothesis (H1) was not supported. H1 had supposed that group consensus and postdiscussion opinions would be affected by information conveyed in the graphics conditions {g} and {g+avg} to a greater extent than in the sentential condition {s}.

H2. GROUP DISCUSSION

Although it also had been postulated that modality might have an effect on discussion duration (H2), data did not support this conjecture, either. Likewise, the total messages for each condition did not vary significantly (H2).

The number of messages occurring during persuasive arguments phases (as a percentage of total messages in each discussion) was significant (p = .006). Likewise, the number of messages involving normative arguments also was significant (p = .0001). However, the number of mes-

Table 3. Summary of results from pilot experiment

Condition	Mean	SD	F	p
Discussion Duration (min.)				
s	7.62	3.29	ns	
g	8.20	4.49		
g+avg	8.64	5.81		
Total Messages				
s	25.91	12.56	ns	
g	26.09	17.59		
g+avg	27.73	19.04		
Choice Shift				
s	4.27	1.21	ns	
g	4.67	2.02		
g+avg	4.18	1.75		
Attitude Polarization				
s	1.30	.58	ns	
g	1.10	.47		
g+avg	1.03	.48		
% Msgs. Normative Arguments				
s	.21	.17	12.412	.0001
g	.38	.13		
g+avg	.08	.12		
% Msgs. Persuasive Arguments				
s	.45	.15	6.066	.006
g	.32	.18		
g+avg	.58	.19		
% Msgs. Consensus Attainment				
s	.34	.13	ns	
g	.30	.13		
g+avg	.34	.17		
Explicit First Advocate				
s	1.82	1.33	6.111	.006
g	.79	1.17		
g+avg	.27	.47		
Implicit First Advocate				
s	2.27	1.42	5.091	.013
g	.94	1.20		
g+avg	.82	.87		

Note: "ns" indicates not significant.

sages involving consensus attainment was not significant. These data confirm parts of hypothesis H2, establishing that the presence of a graphical modality in both {g} and {g+avg} affected discussion structure and content.

More detailed pairwise comparisons ·of the significant

results are summarised in Table 4. There were proportionately more normative arguments in {g} (m = .38) than in {s} (m = .21, p < .01) or in {g+avg} (m = .08, p < .05). Likewise, for {s} there were more normative arguments than in {g+avg} (p < .01). In sum, for normative arguments, proportionately: {g} > {s} > {g+avg}, which supports portions of H2.

Table 4. Pair-wise comparison of significant conditions

Condition	Mean	SD	p
% Msgs. Normative Arguments			
s	.21	.16	.01
g	.38	.13	
s	.21	.16	.01
g+avg	.08	.11	
g	.38	.13	.05
g+avg	.08	.11	
% Msgs. Persuasive Arguments			
s	.45	.14	.1
g	.32	.17	
s	.45	.14	.1
g+avg	.58	.18	
g	.32	.17	.01
g+avg	.58	.18	
Explicit First Advocate			
s	1.82	1.33	.05
g	.79	1.17	
s	1.82	1.33	.01
g+avg	.27	.47	
g	.79	1.17	ns
g+avg	.27	.47	
Implicit First Advocate			
s	2.27	1.42	.05
g	.94	1.20	
s	2.27	1.42	.01
g+avg	.82	.87	
g	.94	1.20	ns
g+avg	.82	.87	

Notes: (1) The Duncan comparison procedure was performed using the SPSS statistical software package.
(2) "ns" indicates not significant.

There were proportionately more persuasive arguments in {g+avg} (m = .58) than in {s} (m = .45, p < .1) or {g} (m = .32, p < .01). There also were more persuasive arguments in {s} than in {g} (p < .1). In sum, for persuasive arguments: {g+avg} > {s} > {g}, which also supports H2.

H3. FIRST ADVOCACY

Regarding H3, significant effects were observed regarding explicit first advocate (p = .006), and implicit first advocate (p = .013). These data support the hypothesis that the explicit and implicit first advocate have greater influence on group consensus in {g} and {g+avg} than in {s}.

Regarding explicit and implicit first advocacy (H3), {g} and {g+avg} did not vary significantly from each other, as predicted. Significant first advocacy results were observed between {s} and {g}, as predicted (explicit p < .05; implicit p < .05), and between {s} and {g+avg} (explicit p < .01; implicit p < .01). The non-significant results in the {s} condition replicate results found in earlier face-to-face and sentential CM research (Weisband, 1992). Tables 5 and 6 summarise actual findings versus those anticipated.

Table 5. Summary of anticipated versus actual findings, group consensus hypotheses (H1, H3)

		Treatment conditions (IVs)					
		No first advocacy			First advocacy		
		g	g+avg	s	g	g+avg	s
Level of accord (averaging effect, DVs)	**high**		x		x		x
	medium	x					
	low						x
	none		x				

Notes: (1) "x" indicates value of anticipated finding for treatment indicated.
(2) "x" indicates anticipated finding was confirmed at a significant level.

6. Discussion

To summarise, the two discourse types *persuasive arguments* and *normative arguments* varied significantly with respect to the three experimental conditions {g},

Table 6.   Summary of anticipated versus actual findings, group discussion hypotheses (H2)

Level of influence			Treatment conditions		
			g	g+avg	s
Normative (opinion)		high	<u>x</u>		
		medium			x
		low		<u>x</u>	
Informational (persuasion)		high		x	
		medium			x
		low	x		

Length of discussion		Treatment conditions		
		g	g+avg	s
	high			x
	medium	x		
	low		x	

Conciseness of content		Treatment conditions		
		g	g+avg	s
	high		x	
	medium	x		
	low			x

Notes: (1) "x" indicates value of anticipated finding for treatment indicated.
(2) "<u>x</u>" indicates anticipated finding was confirmed at a significant level.

{g+avg} and {s}. The third discourse type, *consensus attainment*, occurred in equal proportions for all three conditions. These data suggest that the bulk of modality effects rested exclusively in phases of discussion where group members attempted to resolve substantiated and unsubstantiated opinions, normative influence, decision proposals, inference and logical arguments in order to attain consensus.

In the two graphics conditions, *explicit* and *implicit* first advocates exerted significant effects on outcomes, whereas such effects were not observed in the control condition {s}.

Three parameters are considered central to the ensuing discussion: (a) individual prediscussion opinions, (b) individual opinions voiced during discussion, and (c) group consensus, which invariably emerges during discussion.

6.1 *Relationships between opinions and modalities*

What may be considered of considerable theoretical interest -- keeping cognitive and perceptual salience in mind -- are relationships between the opinions observed and the communication modalities of the three experimental conditions.

First considering the effects of graphical modality {g+avg} on group discourse: Why would groups spend proportionately *less* time discussing opinions and asserting normative influence and proportionately *more* time substantiating their opinions with persuasive arguments, thus asserting more informational influence?

It may be that when group members see each others' opinions as part of the group average {g+avg}, those opinions present an irrefutable implied informational "decision proposal" -- even before discussion begins. The graphical display frames subjects' individual opinions with a salient notion of consensus, denoted by the informational average. With the explicit knowledge that each member eventually will need to adjust personal opinion towards a consensus, s/he will be more motivated to argue. Persuasive arguments grounded in fact, logic and inference will need to be used to justify and protect his/her position. Since individual members are more committed to their positions (further reinforced by their own persuasive arguments), it would not seem logical for them to submit alternate positions. Such self-reinforcement also would explain the small proportion of normative arguments.

Regarding the {g} condition: Why do groups engage in discussion whose proportions are diametrically opposed to those of {g+avg}? It may be that when discussants encounter the {g} graphical display (without explicitly seeing the average ,as in {g+avg}), they may assume that *no* decision proposal has begun to take shape. Discussants have no external reference against which to measure their individual opinions. They are not compelled to defend their positions, nor do they have a salient notion of opinion *and* consensus, as in {g+avg}.

On the contrary, in {g} discussants have a strong notion of their own opinions, and these opinions overshadow any sense of consensus. This situation contributes to a lack of cohesion as discussion begins, and as individual opinions change and the group consensus takes shape. This explains the greater proportions of normative argument.

The effects of {g} also explain the attenuation of persuasive arguments, since discussants are not compelled to justify their opinions (as in {g+avg}).

The "neutral" modality ({s}, a control for the experiment) favoured persuasive arguments over normative arguments. When discussants first announce their prediscussion opinions personally to one another it may be that greater emphasis is placed on the cohesiveness of group opinion. In other words, by stating one's prediscussion opinion in {s}, one is suggesting explicitly a value for group consensus. As in {g+avg}, group members quickly develop a sense of what the consensus value *might* be, thereby inducing a need to justify one's own position, through persuasive argument.

6.2 *First advocacy*

In terms of implicit and explicit first advocacy, both graphics conditions ({g} and {g+avg}) were associated with greater influence on consensus than was the control condition {s}. In both graphics conditions, the cognitively and perceptually salient information from prediscussion graphical feedback ostensibly anchored discussants closer to the value of the first advocate's position. Compared with the sentential condition, this resulted in a significantly smaller shift of opinion from the moment of first advocacy to consensus. Owing to the lack of salience, however, first advocates in {s} discussions did not have as much of an influence on consensus as in the other two conditions. (The notions of "opinion" and "consensus" are more susceptible to working memory effects and the combination of information gleaned from the discourse, resulting in a shift of opinion away from the first advocate.)

What is interesting generally about these results when they are compared with traditional face-to-face research is the clear delineation between normative and informational influence that occurs in most discussions. In some cases a decision proposal might have been appended to what was otherwise a persuasive argument, but in general the distinction between normative and informational was quite clear.

Also of interest were the nearly identical proportions (roughly one-third each) spent in consensus attainment, for all three conditions. The non-significant variances of discussion duration, discussion times, number of messages, choice shift and attitude polarisation also were notable. These aggregate data provided a backdrop against which influence-related parameters could be examined. Further decomposition and classification of discourse types in future research could reveal still more interesting discussion dynamics, as could detailed study of decision rules applied by discussants.

6.3 *Saliences of discussion parameters*

Table 7 presents the relative saliencies of the three parameters (individual prediscussion opinion, individual opinion during the discussion, and group consensus), along with the two significant outcomes: persuasive arguments and normative arguments. The metrics "high", "med", and "low" are assigned loosely to these five elements, in order to denote the relative saliencies associated with (a) the experimental manipulations (the first three columns) and (b) results from content coding of the discussion (the last two columns). Beginning with the row describing {g}, note that saliency of prediscussion opinions (as well as of discussion opinions) are "high" (owing to graphical representation), and that group consensus is "low" (since it develops solely during conversation, under the sentential modality).

For {g+avg}, prediscussion opinions are "high", as in {g}, but discussion opinions and group consensus are "low" and "high", respectively -- effects that are directly opposite to the "high" and "low" of {g}. This dynamic property also is reflected in the proportions of informational/persuasive and normative arguments.

What can be said, therefore, about the effects of salience on group discussion with respect to influence? First, it appears that informational influence can be associated better with aggregate group opinion (consensus) than with individual opinion. Likewise, it seems that normative influence can be associated better with individual opinion than with aggregate opinion.

6.3 *Saliences of first advocacy*

Regarding first advocacy (Table 8), the same experimental conditions (the first three columns) give rise to similar results in terms of the correspondence between an individual's opinion and the *value* (not the formation) of consensus. Opinions unfold temporally, through the course of discussion. The true linear phenomenon of "conversation" therefore should be contrasted with the "clustering of opinion" experience.

7. Conclusions

Empirical results support the conclusion that *communication modality* has significant effects on how CM group members attempt to influence each other during decision-making discussion. When they view 2D graphical information about their prediscussion opinions, group members attempt to assert more *informational influence* on one another.

Effects of combining interactive graphics

Table 7. "Saliency" matrix for discussion parameters

Condition	Prediscussion Opinions	Discussion Opinions	Group Consensus	Persuasive Arguments	Normative Arguments
g	high	high	low	low	high
g+avg	high	low	high	high	low
s	low	low	low	med	med

Table 8. "Saliency" matrix for first advocacy

Condition	Prediscussion Opinions	Discussion Opinions	Group Consensus	Explicit 1st Advocacy	Implicit 1st Advocacy
g	high	high	low	med	med
g+avg	high	low	high	high	med
s	low	low	low	low	low

One is compelled to ask the question, "What constitutes a 'good decision', as opposed to a 'bad decision', in group decision-making". Unfortunately, such issues are highly subjective and context-dependent. But more importantly, it is not the role of the social scientist to ascribe values such as "good" or "bad", or to evaluate "quality" regarding any group's decision-making activities. It is clear, however, that designers of graphics-based displays should be aware that display composition can exacerbate some small group tendencies while attenuating others. Such self-awareness on the part of designers and users is key.

Knowing that members of electronic groups might be susceptible to effects observed in this study, how might such effects bear on loss of inhibition, status equalisation, riskier decision-making, and variations between normative and informational influence -- as they might relate (for example) to the case of Rodney King? Were such potential effects envisioned by the designers of the electronic mail system used in Los Angeles Police patrol cars in connection with that notorious beating incident?

The answer in all likelihood is: probably not. However, given the effects on small group behaviour seen in this study, how might tool designers seek to curtail or avoid inappropriate consensus behaviour?

One approach might be a *pro-active* and empirical design methodology. In such a methodology,

(a) the designer would seek to understand user responses observed in this study in the context of tools being developed,

(b) the designer would design tools which make user responses more salient, perhaps by abstracting salient aspects of such responses in other modalities (like interactive 2D graphics) -- so that design intent is more effectively conveyed to potential users,

(c) the designer would test for exacerbation or attenuation of such effects on the tools' computer-mediated group in a controlled experimental setting, perhaps accompanied by follow-up in the field, and finally,

(d) if effects exceed acceptable criteria (e.g., as detected by analysis groups' conversations), the designer would redesign the tool and repeat this cycle until user responses pass acceptable criteria.

Although such an "action" methodology might raise objections, it is not unlike the "third eye" brake light mechanism that has become a regulated standard in American automobiles. Its integration with existing brake lights was prompted by faulty user responses, which confused braking intent with other rear-end visual cues such as tail lights. This confusion sometimes resulted in rear-end collisions. With addition of the unambiguous "third eye", braking intent was more explicit, resulting in proportionately fewer rear-end collisions. In view of the work I have reported here, I am making a similar case for CM-HCI.

Acknowledgments

Ellice Forman, Stephen Hirtle, Jill Larkin, Alan Lesgold, John Levine, Mike Lewis, Dirk Mahling, Richard Moreland and Walter Schneider. Special thanks to Sara Kiesler for her help in cultivating many of the foundational ideas that have gone into this research. Thanks to the Industrial Networking Institute at Carnegie Mellon and the University of Pittsburgh Department of Information Science for funding the subjects who participated in this study.

References

BRANSFORD, J.D., BARCLAY, J.R., & FRANKS, J.J. 1973, Sentence memory: a constructive versus interpretive approach. *Cognitive Psychology* **3** (1972), 193-209.

FISK, A.D., & LLOYD, S.J. 1988, The role of stimulus-to-rule consistency in learning rapid application of spatial rules. *Human Factors* **30** (1), 35-49.

KAPLAN, S. & SIMON, H. A. 1989, Foundations of cognitive science. In M.I. Posner (ed), *Foundations of Cognitive Science*. (MIT Press, Cambridge, MA).

KIESLER, S. & SPROULL, L. 1992,. Group decision making and communication technology. *Organizational Behavior and Human Decision Processes* **52**, 96-123.

KOTOVSKY, K., HAYES, J.R. & SIMON, H.A. 1985, Why are some problems hard? Evidence from tower of hanoi. *Cognitive Psychology* **17**, 248-294.

LEWIS, C.M., & TOTH, J.A. 1992, Situated cognition in diagrammatic reasoning. In N.H. Narayanan (ed), *Working Notes*, 47-52, AAAI Spring Symposium on Reasoning with Diagrammatic Representations, March 25-27, 1992 (Stanford University, Stanford, CA).

LOFTUS, E.F., MILLER, D.G. & BURNS, H.J. 1978, Semantic integration of verbal information into a visual memory. *Journal of Experimental Psychology: Human Learning and Memory* **4**, 19-31.

MANDLER, J.M. & RITCHEY, G.H. 1977, Long-term memory for pictures. *Journal of Experimental Psychology: Human Learning and Memory* **3**, 386-396.

MILLER, C.E. 1989, The social psychological effects of group decision rules. In P.B. Paulus (ed), *Psychology of Group Influence* (2nd ed), 327-355 (Lawrence Erlbaum Associates, Hillsdale, NJ).

NICKERSON, R. S., & ADAMS, M. J. 1979, Long-term memory for a common object. *Cognitive Psychology* **11**, 287-307.

PAIVIO, A. 1986, Mental representations: a dual coding approach (Oxford University Press, New York).

RIDGEWAY, C.L. 1984, Dominance, performance, and status in groups: a theoretical analysis. In E.J. Lawler (ed), *Advances in Group Processes* **1**, 59-93 (JAI Press, Greenwich, CT).

SCHNEIDER, W. & DETWEILER, M. 1987, A connectionist/control architecture for working memory. In G.H. Bower (ed), *The Psychology of Learning and Motivation 21*, 53-119 (Academic Press, Orlando, FL).

STRAUS, S.G. 1991, Does the Medium Matter: An Investigation of Process, Performance, and Affect in Computer-Mediated and Face-to-Face Groups. Working paper, Graduate School of Industrial Administration, Carnegie Mellon University, Pittsburgh, PA.

TABACHNEK, H. & SIMON, H.A. 1992, Reasoning About economic markets. In N.H. Narayanan (ed), *Working Notes*, 59-64, AAAI Spring Symposium on Reasoning with Diagrammatic Representations, March 25-27, 1992 (Stanford University, Stanford, CA).

VAN ORDEN, G.C., PENNINGTON, B.F. & STONE, G.O. 1990, Word identification in reading and the promise of subsymbolic psycholinguistics. *Psychological Review* **97** (4), 488-522.

WEISBAND, S.P. 1992, Group discussion and first advocacy effects in computer-mediated and face-to-face decision making groups. *Organizational Behavior and Human Decision Processes* **53**, 352-380.

ZHANG, J. & NORMAN, D.A. 1990, The Interaction of Internal and External Information in a Problem-Solving Task. Technical Report 9005, Dept. of Cognitive Science, University of California/San Diego, La Jolla, CA.

Postscript

A convergence of disciplines

One indicator of the degree to which there is in fact a confluence of interests and research focus on this topic is the frequency with which contributors cited the same authors in two or more papers. These mutual references form the core of a body of literature addressing some aspect of the special issue theme.

BODKER, S. & GRONBAEK, K. 1991, Cooperative prototyping: users and designers in mutual activity. In J. Greenbaum & M. Kyng (eds), *Design At Work: Cooperative Design of Computer Systems* (Lawrence Erlbaum Associates, Hillsdale, NJ).

BODKER, S. 1991, *Through the Interface Systems* (Lawrence Erlbaum Associates, Hillsdale, NJ).

BOWERS, J., & CHURCHER, J. 1988, Local and global structuring of computer mediated communication: developing linguistic perspectives on CSCW in COSMOS. *CSCW Proceedings 1988*, 125-139.

BOWERS, J.M., BENFORD, S.D. (eds) 1991, *Studies in Computer Supported Cooperative Work: Theory, Practice and Design* (North-Holland, Amsterdam).

CARD, S. K., MORAN, T. P. & NEWELL, A. 1983, *The Psychology of Human-Computer Interaction* (Lawrence Erlbaum Associates, Hillsdale, NJ).

GALEGHER, J. & KRAUT, R. 1990, Technology for intellectual teamwork: Perspectives on research and design. In Galegher, J., Kraut, R., & Egido, C. (eds), *Intellectual Teamwork*, 1-20 (Lawrence Erlbaum Associates, Hillsdale, NJ).

GENTNER, D. & STEVENS, A.L. (eds) 1983, *Mental Models* (Lawrence Erlbaum Associates, Hillsdale, NJ).

JOHNSON, P. & NICOLOSI, E. 1990, Task-based user interface development tools. In D. Diaper et al (eds), *Proceedings of the Third IFIP TC13 Conference on Human-Computer Interaction Interact'90*, 383-387 (North-Holland, Amsterdam).

JOHNSON-LAIRD, P. N. 1983, *Mental Models*. (Cambridge University Press Cambridge, UK).

JOHNSON-LAIRD, P.N. 1985, Mental models. In Aitkenhead, A.M., & Slack, J.M. (eds), *Issues in Cognitive Modeling* (Lawrence Erlbaum Associates, Ltd., Sussex, UK).

LEWIS, C. 1986, Understanding what's happening in system interactions. In D. A. Norman & S.W. Draper (eds), *User Centred System Design*, 169-185 (Lawrence Erlbaum Associates, Hillsdale, NJ).

LEWIS, C. M., & TOTH, J. A. 1992, Situated Cognition in Diagrammatic Reasoning. In N.H. Narayanan (ed), *Working Notes, AAAI Spring Symposium on Reasoning with Diagrammatic Representations*, 47- 52. (March 25-27, 1992). (Stanford University, Stanford, CA).

MORAN, T. P. AND ANDERSON, R. J. 1990, The workaday world as a paradigm for CSCW design. *Proceedings of the Conference on Computer-Supported Cooperative Work*, 381-393. (October 7-10, 1990). (ACM, Los Angeles).

NICKERSON, R. S. 1976, On conversational interaction with computers. In R.M. Baecker & W.A.S. Buxton (eds) (1987), *Readings in Human Computer Interaction*, 681-693 (Morgan Kaufmann Los Altos, CA).

NICKERSON, R.S., & ADAMS, M.J. 1979, Long-term memory for a common object. *Cognitive Psychology* 11, 287-307.

NORMAN, D. A. 1983, Some observations on mental models. In D. Gentner & A. Stevens (eds), *Mental Models* (Lawrence Erlbaum Associates, Hillsdale, NJ).

NORMAN, D. A. 1987, Cognitive artifacts. In J.M. Carroll (ed), *Interfacing Thought*, 17-38 (MIT Press, Cambridge, MA).

NORMAN, D. A. 1988, *The Psychology of Everyday Things* (Basic Books, New York).

SUCHMAN, L. & TRIGG, R. 1991, Understanding practice: Video as a medium for reflection and design. In J. Greenbaum & M. Kyng (eds), *Design At Work: Cooperative Design of Computer Systems* (Lawrence Erlbaum Associates, Hillsdale, NJ).

SUCHMAN, L. A. 1987, *Plans and Situated Actions: The Problem of Human-Computer Communication*. (Cambridge University Press, Cambridge, UK).

WINOGRAD T. AND FLORES, C. F. 1986, *Understanding Computers and Cognition: A New Foundation for Design* (Addison-Wesley, Reading, MA).

WINOGRAD, T. 1986, A language/action perspective on the design of cooperative work. *CSCW Proceedings 1986*, 203-220 (ACM, New York).

WINOGRAD, T. 1987, A language/action perspective on the design of cooperative work. *Human Computer Interaction* 3, 3-30.

Index

A

abduction, 37, 40, 43
activity cycle diagrams, 69, 70
adaptation, 33, 71
adaptive structuration, viii, 57, 59, 61, 64
adoption, 57, 58, 65
animation, 16
appropriation, 16, 29, 32, 39, 40, 52, 58, 59, 60, 61, 64, 71, 80
artificial intelligence, 29, 32, 34, 35, 38
artificial visual systems, 46
attention, 16, 19, 21, 22, 23, 24, 28, 39, 67, 75, 76
attitude polarisation, 82

B

Balint, Lajos, v, viii, 28
bandwidth, 13, 14
behavioural spirit, 62
belief systems, 58
Bush, Vannevar, 38

C

capacity dimension, 50
cartography, 39, 40
catalysts, 33
choice shift, 77, 82, 85
cognition, v, vii, viii, 31, 35, 45, 47, 49, 52, 53, 54, 68, 75, 76, 87
cognitive communication, v, 15
cognitive complexity, 49
cognitive fit, vii, ix
cognitive maps, 45, 46, 47, 48, 52, 53
collaboration, v, viii, 15, 16, 18, 21, 22, 23, 24, 25, 26, 31, 32, 39, 41, 57, 59, 60, 61, 62, 63, 65, 66, 70
collectivism, 59
communicative practices, 16, 22, 23, 24, 26
community of practice, 23
computer-supported cooperative work (CSCW), 57
conjectures, 24
conscious awareness, 46
consensus, 63, 74, 76, 77, 78, 79, 80, 81, 82, 83, 84, 85, 86
constraints, vi, 15, 20, 40, 63, 64, 65, 67, 68
context, viii, 14, 16, 21, 22, 23, 29, 32, 34, 38, 39, 41, 52, 59, 60, 61, 62, 63, 64, 65, 68, 71, 73, 74, 75, 86
convergence, 88
conversation paradigm, 11
coordination theory, 62, 63
coping, 20, 22

coupling, 22, 78
culture, 20, 39, 41
customisation, 62, 63, 64, 65

D

Day, Donald, iii, ix
decision-making, viii, 47, 55, 62, 65, 66, 67, 68, 76, 77, 84, 85, 87
decoding/encoding, 28, 29, 32, 33
denotational relationship, 24
designers, 11, 14, 15, 16, 21, 24, 26, 34, 37, 38, 39, 41, 42, 43, 44, 57, 58, 59, 67, 68, 72, 75, 86, 88
deterministic, 60, 61, 62
digital video technology, viii
digitising glass tablet, 52
dimensionality, 47, 49, 52
direct manipulation, 11, 14, 15, 16, 17, 33
direct observation, 49, 50
discourse, 80, 81
display composition, 86
distance learning, 39
dynamic intermediaries, 68, 71

E

effects of scale, 48
Electronic Journal on Virtual Culture, vi
electronic media, 11, 12, 13, 14, 60, 75, 86
emergence, 47, 59, 60
engagement, 16, 22
expert, viii, 15, 16, 17, 19, 20, 21, 22, 24, 25, 26
explicit decision proposal, 81
explicit sense, 39

F

fidelity, v, viii, 14, 15, 16, 17, 18, 19, 20, 21, 22, 23, 24, 25, 32, 33
filtering, 28, 29, 31, 33
first advocacy, 74, 78, 83, 84, 85, 86
formalism, 30, 33, 34
fractal, viii, 45, 46, 47, 48, 49, 50, 51, 52, 53, 54, 55
frames, 40, 84
fulfilment, 42
Fuller, Buckminster, viii, 37, 40, 43
Fuller, Rodney, v, vii, 11

G

gender differences, 53, 79
Gentry, Tom, ii, v, 45
geographic information systems, 47
gesture, 23, 26, 33
graphics, viii, 17, 42, 47, 74, 75, 76, 77, 78, 79, 80, 82, 84, 85, 86
group behaviour, 60, 61, 75, 77
group consensus, 76, 77, 78, 79, 81, 82, 83, 84, 85
group decision support systems (GDSS), vii, 57, 58, 59, 60, 61, 63, 64, 65, 66

H

holistic approach, 41, 42
human brain function, asymmetry of, 52
human imagination, geometry of, 45
hypertext, viii, 37, 38, 39, 41

I

IDEAbase, 37, 39, 40, 41, 43, 44
implicit sense, 39
information transfer, 28, 29, 31, 32, 33, 34, 35, 61, 62, 63
informational influence, 77, 78, 84, 85, 86
inquiry, v, viii, 15, 16, 18, 20, 21, 22, 23, 24, 25, 26, 40
intelligent processing, 32
Interactive determinism, 59
interdependencies, 63
intermediaries, v, vii, 31, 32, 33, 47, 48, 68, 70, 71
internalisation, 16, 21
Internet Relay Chat, 79
interpersonal communication, v, 11, 28, 29
interpretation, 16, 18, 24, 33, 34, 59, 65, 78
interviews, 18, 41, 72
isolation, 76, 79
iterated equations, 47

J

judgement, 24, 37, 38

K

Kern, Krista, v, 45
knowledge base, 29, 32, 34
knowledge structures, 16
Kovacs, Diane, iii, ix

L

learning, 15, 16, 20, 21, 22, 24, 25, 26, 38, 39, 43, 52, 87
lifeworld, 62, 63
linguistics, vii, 23, 26, 29, 33, 34, 38, 46, 47, 48, 62, 66, 73, 75, 76, 88

M

Mandviwalla, Munir, viii, ix, 57
mapping, viii, 37, 38, 40, 43, 46, 47, 53, 54, 68, 77
mediated collaborative inquiry, viii, 15, 16, 18, 21, 25
mediation, 42, 74, 75
mental maps, v, vii, viii, 47, 49
mental models, vii, viii, 12, 15, 16, 17, 19, 20, 21, 22, 23, 24, 25, 28, 29, 32, 33, 38, 45, 53, 65, 67, 68, 69
metaphor, 17, 20, 23, 26, 42, 62
microworlds, 21
modalities, 75, 76, 84, 86
modelling, 37, 38, 40, 42, 67, 68, 69, 70, 71, 72, 73
Moose, Phil, v, 45
motor behaviours, 46, 49

N

negotiation, 58, 64, 65
neural networks, 47
neurological disorders, 48
nomic processing, 75, 76
nonlinear analysis, 45
nonlinear geometric models, 47
normative arguments, 81, 82, 83, 84, 85
normative influence, 77, 78, 84, 85

O

Object Lens, 63, 64
organisational change, 60
orientation, 48, 50, 53

P

paradigmatic pluralism, 64
participatory design, 25
Paul, Ray, viii, 67, 71
perception, vii, 11, 16, 30, 40, 47, 53, 54, 63, 75, 76
personality, 11, 12, 13, 45, 49, 53
persuasive arguments, 74, 76, 80, 81, 82, 83, 84, 85
Petri nets, 70
placement, 18, 24, 60
pointing behaviour, viii, 23, 45, 46, 47, 48, 49, 50, 51, 52, 53, 54, 62
power function, 45, 50, 52
problem communication, 69
problem formulation, 69, 70
problem representation, vii, viii, 15, 16, 19, 21, 22, 25, 40, 42, 43, 45, 46, 47, 48, 54, 67, 69, 70, 71, 75, 77, 87
process losses, 61
propositional models, 38
protocol, 17, 76
psychometric measures, 45, 51, 52

Q

quality of work life, 61
questionnaires, 12, 13, 49, 78, 80

R

rapid prototyping, 25
received wisdom, 37
receiving matrix, 40
relationships, viii, 13, 18, 20, 22, 25, 28, 30, 37, 39, 40, 52, 53, 57, 63, 68, 84
response specification, 48
restrictiveness, 65
reviewers, ix
rhetoric, 38, 41
Roschelle, Jeremy, v, viii, 15

S

scaling, 18, 46, 52
schemata, 40, 48, 54
scholastic rigour, 38
scripts, 40
semantics, 14, 33, 39, 43, 62, 75, 76, 80
semiotics, 46
sensing, 19
sentential messages, 74
sentential text, 75, 77
shared meaning, 16, 23, 31
shared workspace, 62, 66
simulation, viii, 16, 17, 22, 23, 24, 25, 67, 68, 69, 70, 71, 72, 73
situated context, 24, 34
sketch maps, viii, 45, 48, 49, 50, 51, 53
small groups, 75, 79
social cognitions, 12
social context cues, 14, 74
social influence, viii, 74
social interaction, 12, 60
software tools, v, vii, viii, 12, 21, 22, 23, 28, 29, 31, 32, 33, 39, 47, 57, 62, 63, 64, 67, 68, 70, 71, 72, 86, 88
source mapping, 38
spatial awareness, 42

spatial cognition, v, viii, 45, 46, 47, 48, 49, 51, 53, 54
specification methods, 70
Speech Act Theory, 62
stakeholders, 67, 68
Strueland, Teri, v
syllogistic logic, 37
synchronisation, 23, 62

T

Taylor, Paul, v, viii, 37, 39
Technological determinism, 59, 60
Technological emergence, 59, 60
Thomas, Peter, viii, 67
topographical features, 62
Toth, Jozsef, viii, 74
transformation, 21, 22
triangulation analysis techniques, 18

U

Utopianism, 60

V

video interaction analysis, 25
view compatibility, 58
view focus, 58, 62, 63
view independence, 58
view source, 58
visual perception, 54
visualisation, 17, 21

W

wicked problems, 40
Wood, John, v, viii, 37
work method, 43
workaday world, 14, 66, 88
working memory effects, 85
world view, v, vii, viii, 15, 16, 19, 21, 24, 25, 26, 57, 58, 59, 60, 61, 62, 63, 64, 65, 66

Printed and bound by CPI Group (UK) Ltd, Croydon, CR0 4YY

22/10/2024

01777391-0004